THAT CRAZY
LITTLE THING CALLED
LOVE

THAT CRAZY
LITTLE THING CALLED
LOVE

THE SOUNDTRACK OF MARRIAGE, SEX, AND FAITH

JUD WILHITE

Standard®
PUBLISHING
Bringing The Word to Life

Cincinnati, Ohio

Published by Standard Publishing, Cincinnati, Ohio
www.standardpub.com

© 2007 Jud Wilhite

Printed in China

Project editor: Laura Derico
Cover and interior design: studiogearbox.com
Author photo: Davy Knapp

ISBN 0-7847-1944-6

13 12 11 10 09 08 07   9 8 7 6 5 4 3 2 1

Library of Congress Cataloging-in-Publication Data

Wilhite, Jud, 1971-
  That crazy little thing called love : the soundtrack of marriage, sex, and
faith / Jud Wilhite.
      p. cm.
  ISBN 0-7847-1944-6 (casebound with jacket)
  1. Bible. O.T. Song of Solomon--Criticism, interpretation, etc. 2.
Marriage--Biblical teaching. 3. Love--Biblical teaching. I. Title.

BS1485.52.W55 2007
248.8'44--dc22

2006028599

To Lori

For more than words can say

THE SOUNDTRACK

FOREWORD

On the wall in Jud Wilhite's office is a spectacular picture of Las Vegas; the lights of Sin City spread out below a sheltering mountain range. And on the picture, superimposed above and behind the mountain range, are two massive words: Grace City.

You see, Jud pastors the 10,000-member Central Christian Church in Las Vegas, and he has seen firsthand that there is no place that the grace of God cannot reach, no sin that cannot be redeemed, no relationship that cannot be restored. Pastoring in one of the least-churched, most desperately in-need cities in this country, Jud has been powerfully used by God to bring the unconditional, nonjudgmental love of Jesus to people who know little or nothing about him. And he's done it not by trying to escape from the culture, but by speaking its language; not by avoiding the challenging truths of the Bible, but by putting them into a context that is easily understood, compelling, and fun!

As you page through *That Crazy Little Thing Called Love,* you will get a full blast from the sneakily insightful Jud Wilhite. Who knew that a marriage devotional could be so compelling that you would want to read it like a novel?

One reason this little book stands out is that Jud opens the eyes of husbands and wives to things we have probably never seen or understood about each other, and does it in so many different ways that it stays fresh and interesting. He takes us on an absorbing tour through the Song of Solomon, using scientific studies, pop-culture factoids, and even the insights of such songwriter philosophers as Bono and Kenny Rogers to illustrate points about marriage that were first made thousands of years ago in the Bible.

As you walk through this devotional, I'll bet you'll have the same sense of surprise and wonder that I did at how the Song of Solomon comes alive as a totally understandable road map for navigating the challenges and joys of marriage. And you too will see that there is no place that the grace of God cannot reach.

Enjoy the journey!

SHAUNTI FELDHAHN

Best-selling author of *For Women Only: What You Need to Know About the Inner Lives of Men* and coauthor of *For Men Only: A Straightforward Guide to the Inner Lives of Women*

ACKNOWLEDGMENTS

I'm grateful for so many whose friendship and skill have helped this book along. My wife, Lori, is always encouraging and supportive. Thanks for being my best friend and date for life. To my kids, Emma and Ethan, thanks for pulling Dad off the computer to wrestle, for reminding me of what is really important in life, and for infusing my life with so much joy. Carlos and Mary Wilhite along with Jimmy and Carolyn Williams have modeled great marriages and taught me so much through their actions. Thanks for your faithfulness and courage.

Some of my favorite times in developing content from the Song of Solomon were sitting with Michael Murphy and Justin Jackson, sharing ideas, thoughts, and creativity. Thanks for your input and insight. I appreciate Jon Kohler, Karen Englert, and Dianna Melson for their expertise and ideas. Karen, thanks for the idea of the song titles! A huge thank-you to Eugena Kelting for keeping everything in my life on track. Much love to my friends, named and unnamed, who make the journey worthwhile—Mike and Lisa Bodine, the Central Church and staff, Mike and Jenn Foster, the McGowan clan, John and Marsha Ketchen, Todd and Andrea Stephens, Chris and Christy Ferebee, everyone at PTCC and Crossroads, Greg and Julie Nettle, Barry and Gaye McMurtrie—thanks for your love and support. I appreciate Dale Reeves and the team at Standard Publishing for your invaluable work and encouragement.

The soundtrack I listened to while writing this book ranged from Louis Armstrong to Rich Mullins, U2, Amos Lee, Elton John, and Switchfoot. Thanks for the inspiration through music. I'm grateful to the Righteous Brothers for "Unchained Melody," which the band played perfectly the night I proposed, and to Aunt Betsy for "Date for Life," which was sung at our wedding by my dear friends Rob and Shannon Maupin. Late nights writing were accompanied by Intelligentsia coffee—thanks for your Black Cat Blend, and to Isomac for making a great espresso machine . . . since 1977.

Much gratitude to you for reading this book and allowing me to share in your life. That is an honor I cherish. I pray that in reading it you receive a fraction of what I did in writing it. Keep lookin' up.

Crazy Little Thing Called Love

Love has a way of making you sing. I'll never forget blurting out "I love you" for the first time to my future wife, Lori, in the McDonald's parking lot of Plainview, Texas. After she affirmed her love, I gave her a quick kiss, said I would call soon, and jumped in my car. As I drove home my heart soared at the thought of her love. I rivaled Sinatra (with strep throat) in my vocal acrobatics! Thankfully, no one else could hear me.

There's no shortage of love songs. Breaking up, making up, and falling in love are pivotal life experiences. It's enough to drive you crazy. Maybe that's why Freddie Mercury of the band Queen wrote "Crazy Little Thing Called Love" at a Hilton in Munich as he tried to relax in a hot bath. The song's sound is a tribute to Elvis, but its message is universal. It's country music, though, that produces the best relationship song titles. What other form of music could churn out lyrics such as "Get your tongue out of my mouth because I'm kissing you good-bye," or "Get out the meatballs, Momma, we're coming to a fork in the road"? And here's a classic from the '50s: "How could you believe me when I said I loved you when you know I've been a liar all my life?"

Love songs have been around as long as people have been in love. Three thousand years ago, King Solomon was inspired by his bride to write a love song. Solomon was the king of Israel from 971 to 931 BC. He assumed the throne at age twenty and reigned for forty years in peace. Solomon wrote 3,000 proverbs and 1,005 psalms (1 Kings 4:32). But according to this prolific writer himself, his crowning glory is a love song, the Song of Solomon. He begins it by writing "The Song, best of all songs, Solomon's song" (1:1, The Message). This is not just any song, but the best song, his masterpiece. And this song is a Cinderella story.

My four-year-old daughter has watched *Cinderella* so many times I have large sections of it memorized. She plays with Cinderella toys, slippers, and dress-up clothes. One day she came downstairs dressed up as Cinderella with Spider-Man gloves on. Somehow, they fit together perfectly in her world. When she is ready for bed she says, "Dad, carry me upstairs like a princess." So I scoop her up like a princess and carry her upstairs.

FREDDIE MERCURY OF THE BAND QUEEN WROTE "CRAZY LITTLE THING CALLED LOVE" AT A HILTON IN MUNICH AS HE TRIED TO RELAX IN A HOT BATH.

Did you know there are over 1,500 different versions of the Cinderella story? The versions vary around the world, but usually center around a prince who falls in love with a peasant girl. Love enables them to conquer all their differences. The Cinderella story is ingrained in our culture. Even come-from-behind sports teams are called Cinderella teams. But the oldest Cinderella story that I know is found in the Bible. The Song of Solomon is a Cinderella story.

Once upon a time in the hill country of Ephraim, there was a prince. He leased out a vineyard to a family. The parents apparently had died, leaving two brothers to oversee at least two sisters. The brothers treated the girls harshly; they enlisted one in hard labor in the vineyard. One day this young woman met a shepherd. Over time, she and the shepherd developed a friendship that grew into love. The shepherd had to go away, but promised to come back and take the young woman's hand in marriage. He was gone for a long time. The brothers were skeptical. Then the young girl received a summons to visit the palace. She had no idea why she was summoned, but she had to go. Taking a deep breath, she entered the throne room and bowed before the royalty. Then she heard a familiar voice. She raised her head and saw the shepherd, who was actually a prince of Israel. He has called her to be his bride. This is the story of the Song of Solomon.[1]

SOME STUDIES NOW PLACE THE DIVORCE RATE AT 67 PERCENT FOR FIRST MARRIAGES, AND 77 PERCENT FOR SECOND MARRIAGES.

The Song of Solomon is a love song presented in the form of poetry. It is written from three different perspectives: Solomon's, his bride's, and that of a group called the daughters of Jerusalem, who offer a refrain throughout the song. Through these viewpoints, the song reveals the interaction between the king and his wife, dealing with the joys and challenges of marriage and sexual love. The Bible doesn't tell us the woman's name. In 6:13 she is referred to as a Shulammite. In the Hebrew language, *Shulammite* is the feminine word for *Solomon*. This is the story of Mr. and Mrs. Solomon.[2]

Solomon wrote these words as a young man committed to a relationship. He was married and had a son named Rehoboam with his wife Naamah the year before he became king (see 1 Kings 14:21, 31; 2 Chronicles 12:13). In the ancient world, a king would engage in political marriages, taking a wife from another country's royal family to bind the two nations together in alliance. Later Solomon did this too, disobeying the specific command of God and taking 700 wives and 300 concubines. No sons are mentioned as coming from any of Solomon's wives but Naamah, and some interpreters deduce from this that Naamah was his first and ultimate love. They suggest the Song of Solomon is a love song to Naamah.[3] Yet this is only speculation. Later in life Solomon challenged each man to remain true to the wife of his youth. He learned the hard way the valuable lessons of faithfulness and commitment.

There are love songs for every age in every genre, but the Song of Solomon inspires us to navigate love with passion. We spend years of effort in college or trade school to train for careers we may have for a fraction of our lives. Yet, with little or no biblical training in relationships, we stand before God and others and commit to one person for a *lifetime*. Though God has given us an entire book on this subject in the Song of Solomon, few have heard of the book and fewer have studied it. As a result of not understanding God's design for marriage, we may experience years of unnecessary marital frustration. Some studies now place the divorce rate at 67 percent for first marriages, and 77 percent for second marriages. These numbers should shock us and motivate us to learn more about relationships.

I have found the Song of Solomon to be life changing. Its words remind me to pursue my wife as I did before we married. The level of passion between Solomon and his wife challenges me. I am inspired by their marital highs and sympathetic to their lows. I remember that marriage is challenging, but I am not alone.

I've seen the principles in the Song of Solomon transform hundreds of marriages, and I believe they could transform yours, if you apply them. In the following pages we'll progress through the Song. In the first section we'll discuss the importance of remembering your story. We'll look at sharing respect, love, fun, and open communication. In section two, we'll examine Solomon's wedding. We'll draw out principles for fulfilling our marriage vows after we say "I do." Sexual love is the theme of section three. We'll learn about the differences between men and women and discover God's perspective on sex. Healthy conflict resolution is the theme of section four. We'll see how Solomon and his wife deal with conflict, and we'll discover strategies for our own lives. In the final section, we'll find insights from the last chapters of the Song of Solomon on going the distance in a marriage.

If your marriage is barely hanging on, these principles will encourage you to take steps toward a better future together. If your relationship is healthy, they will enhance and enrich what you already have. If you want to learn from a biblical picture of marriage, if you long for romance and passion to return to your relationship, if you desire principles to help you face conflict, turn to the Song of Solomon. Unlike the tune "Fifty Ways to Leave Your Lover," Solomon's song will provide many ways to take your relationship to a new level. In the process you may fall in love all over again.

Will you commit to your partner to read each short chapter and invest in your relationship?

PLAYLIST No. 1

LOVE IS A CRAZY THING

Beautiful

I picked up the phone and took a deep breath. My heart beat fast, and my palms felt moist. I wasn't sure what to say. I had never met Lori Williams, but I knew her family and I had admired her from a distance for a while. The first time I saw her, I was speaking and she was in the audience. When our eyes met, I completely lost my train of thought. Later I heard she was home from college for spring break and would be doing a summer internship at the church I served. I couldn't help but ask her out. So I exhaled and dialed the number. Her mom answered, at first a little cold, thinking I was a credit card salesman. When she realized I was not trying to sell her on American Express, she promised to have Lori return my call. Within an hour Lori called, and I dropped my pickup line: "Lori, I was just, uh, calling to see, uh, if I could, uh, take you out for coffee to encourage you." It is probably the lamest pickup line ever used, but it worked! Our meeting lasted several hours, and the rest is history.

Every couple has a "How did you meet?" story. There's something magical about the story of two separate lives coming together and starting a new life. Throughout your whole life as a couple, whenever someone asks that question, you get to share your story. Picture it. She looks at him and he looks at her, both knowing the story so well. Then one launches into the tale with the other interjecting along the way. Do you know what makes that story so special? It's the very moment their lives intersected for the first time. It's the moment when his life story and her life story intertwined and a whole new chapter began. Neither person would be the same ever again. It's the first story of many they will share together.

We've seen how the Song of Solomon opens, but to get a picture of that initial encounter between Solomon and his wife, we have to turn to the epilogue of the book. In fact, think of this love song as a box of old photos. The two people are reflecting, as if pulling out the photos of their lives and sharing the memories. They go picture by picture through the collection and give a narrative of each one. They are already married at the beginning of the book. In the opening passage she says, "Take me away with you—let us hurry! Let the king bring me into his chambers" (1:4). The king's "chambers" represent a place of intimate physical union. So we can assume that we're introduced to them after their courtship and marriage.

At the end of the book we find the "How did you meet?" question answered. She says, "Solomon had a vineyard in Baal Hamon; he let out his vineyard to tenants. Each was to bring for its fruit a thousand shekels of silver. But my own vineyard is mine to give; the thousand shekels are for you, O Solomon, and two hundred are for those who tend its fruit" (8:11, 12). This couple first met in a vineyard that Solomon leased to her brothers. The tenants made twenty-five pounds of silver for the owner (a thousand shekels) and each one received five pounds of wages (two hundred shekels). Early in the Song of Solomon we learn that she worked in this vineyard under her brothers' care and discipline (1:6). There she met Solomon and fell in love with him.

Remember that crazy time when you fell head over heels for one another? You were suddenly saying things you never thought you'd say, eating food you never thought you'd eat, wearing clothes you never thought you'd wear. When Lori and I were dating, we'd go to the mall.

In my mind, we were just hanging out. In hers, we were on a mission.

As we walked by a store, she said, "Look at that shirt, it would look great on you. It's your color."

"My color?" I replied. "I didn't know I *had* a color. I don't like that shirt; it's not my style."

"No, Jud. You'd look so good in it. Just try it on."

"I'm not trying on the shirt," I said. "And that is that!"

Five minutes later I walked out of the dressing room wearing the shirt.

"Oh, Jud," she said, "that shirt looks so good on you. You need to buy it."

"I'm not buying this shirt. It's bad enough that I tried it on. No way." Then, as if in a stupor, I found myself at the cash register with my wallet out, buying the shirt. That's how love works. It's crazy.

THERE'S SOMETHING MAGICAL ABOUT THE STORY OF TWO SEPARATE LIVES COMING TOGETHER AND STARTING A NEW LIFE.

Yet those early days are also beautiful. They are filled with emotion and eagerness. The tune that captured how I felt about Lori in those days was Billy Corgan's "Beautiful." It describes the warmth of love and companionship in a smooth and melodic way—"with my face pressed up to the glass, wanting you / beautiful, you're beautiful, as beautiful as the sky." I recorded it for her and dropped it in the mail with a sappy letter. I was swirling in the emotions of love.

Thousands of years ago someone wrote, "There are three things that are too amazing for me, four that I do not understand; the way of an eagle in the sky, the way of a snake on a rock, the way of a ship on the high seas, and *the way of a man with a maiden*" (Proverbs 30:18, emphasis added). Things haven't changed much since then. There's still a lot we don't understand about relationships. The early days of love wear off, and we are left trying to understand why we aren't communicating, or being intimate, or getting along.

In the Song of Solomon, we see a couple who have passionate highs and tough lows. They are far from perfect. They struggle, argue, and disagree, but their love remains intact. They are committed to one another. No matter how difficult things become, they reflect positively on the early days of their relationship.

A relationship begins deteriorating when a couple rewrites their history negatively. She recalls their first meeting and focuses on the fact that he was late. He remembers their wedding day and how she fell asleep just after arriving at the hotel. If this rewriting is a tendency you are noticing in your relationship, it is time to step back and evaluate.

"I'VE FOUND 94 PERCENT OF THE TIME THAT COUPLES WHO PUT A POSITIVE SPIN ON THEIR MARRIAGE'S HISTORY ARE LIKELY TO HAVE A HAPPY FUTURE AS WELL."

Dr. John Gottman is a pioneer in the scientific study of marriage. For over twenty years this University of Washington professor has operated what he calls the Love Lab. More than 3,000 different couples have come to the lab, which is an apartment wired up with cameras and microphones. Gottman videotapes these couples' dialogues and then analyzes them according to a system he developed with over twenty categories for every conceivable emotional response, from defensiveness to whining to stonewalling. Everything is explored—facial expressions, body language, tone of voice, and pauses. Physical data from electrodes and sensors is also factored in, revealing when a woman's heartbeat increased, or when a man's temperature rose.

From analyzing this data for one hour, Gottman has a 95 percent accuracy rate at determining whether the couple will be married in fifteen years. After just fifteen minutes, he can determine their future at a 90 percent accuracy rate. Some team members have found significant accuracy after watching a couple dialogue for only three minutes! From his research he writes, "I've found 94 percent of the time that couples who put a positive spin on their marriage's history are likely to have a happy future as well."[4] This is one of the early signs Gottman looks for, because how we view our past determines much about our future.

We live through the stories we tell. We've seen how Solomon met the Shulammite, but when was the last time you told the story of how you first met your spouse? Think of your story again. Remember the things you loved about him or her. Reflect on what drew you together. Share the positive things in your history. Let the telling of your story be the thread that holds you together. By thinking positively about those early days, we realize that we can create our own magical moments whether we have been together for five years or fifty. And that is beautiful.

Over the next few days, look for the opportunity to share your story.

R-E-S-P-E-C-T

You gotta love Aretha. Her powerful voice commanding "R-E-S-P-E-C-T" has captured millions of people, especially women, who have embraced that song as a personal anthem. Just like the Queen of Soul herself, women deserve and desire respect from their mates. And while respect is important for women, it's even more important for men. In fact, the song "R-E-S-P-E-C-T" was first written by a man named Otis Redding. Two years before Aretha recorded it, he released it as a single to send a message to his wife.[5]

In the Song of Solomon, it's immediately apparent that Solomon's wife has great respect for him. This is displayed in the opening passage of the book when she says, "Let him kiss me with the kisses of his mouth—for your love is more delightful than wine. Pleasing is the fragrance of your perfumes; your name is like perfume poured out. No wonder the maidens love you!" (1:2, 3).

Remember, this is poetry. It is not like reading an article in the *New York Times*. There's a lot of flowery language, metaphors, and symbolism. Men in the Old Testament didn't bathe for several days at a time. They put on oil or perfume that would give them a fragrance. So the woman is saying, "Solomon, you smell so good. You're irresistible!" (By the way, I heard a woman on a radio show say that the most annoying thing about men is that too many believe deodorant alone is enough!)

The Shulammite says Solomon not only smells wonderfully but his "name is like perfume poured out." A person's name in the Old Testament stood for his character and reputation. She is saying, "Your name is so valuable it's like expensive perfume poured out. It's a sweet fragrance." These words drip with respect.

AN AMAZING 74 PERCENT OF MEN SAID IF THEY HAD TO CHOOSE, THEY WOULD CHOOSE TO BE ALONE AND UNLOVED RATHER THAN DISRESPECTED!

In his book *Love and Respect*, Dr. Emerson Eggerichs writes about the importance of respect in a man's life. He cites a study in which 400 men were asked to choose between being alone and unloved or being disrespected by everyone. An amazing 74 percent of men said if they had to choose, they would choose to be alone and unloved rather than disrespected![6]

Thousands of years ago, the Bible addressed the issue of man's need for respect. In his letter to the Ephesians, we read this instruction from Paul: "Each one of you also must love his wife as he loves himself, and the wife must respect her husband" (5:33). Notice this passage does not call on husbands and wives to love each other. It charges husbands to *love* their wives, and wives to *respect* their husbands. God knows that a woman's primary need is to feel loved, but a man's primary need is to feel respected. Respect surpasses love and everything else as his most essential need.

Eggerichs cites one woman who says, "Just a few days ago, I decided to tell my husband that I respect him. It felt so awkward to say the words, but I went for it and the reaction was unbelievable! He asked me why I respected him. I listed off a few things, although I could have said many more, and I watched his demeanor change right before my very eyes!"[7] Most women would be surprised at how powerful the words "I respect you" are to a man.

Too often in marriage relationships, we think *love* should be unconditional but *respect*, earned. That may be true in our professional relationships, but in a marriage or dating relationship, men need unconditional respect and women need unconditional love. It does little good to withhold love or respect until your partner seems worthy of it. Rather, respect him and love her regardless, and you may see him or her change before your eyes. The German poet and philosopher Johann Wolfgang von Goethe put it this way, "If you treat a man as he is he will stay as he is. But if you treat him as if he were what he ought to be and could be, he will become that bigger and better man."

One action that causes your partner to feel disrespected is nagging. Nagging may make a person think, *I'm respected at work—they don't nag me there. My friends respect me. I'm respected everywhere I go except for my own home.* Many men especially feel this way, so be careful to show respect for one another. Check yourself when you're tempted to nag. I know, he or she may be well deserving of your reminders. But no matter how justified you feel in bringing some subject up, stop yourself. Your demonstration of respect will transform the way your partner communicates love to you.

MEN NEED UNCONDITIONAL RESPECT AND WOMEN NEED UNCONDITIONAL LOVE.

Women can learn from the Shulammite on this point. Look for things you respect about your husband and share those feelings with him. Make a list of the things you respect and admire about him. You can do this mentally or write them down. Do you respect him for his honesty and integrity? Is it the way he parents his children? Do you respect his intellect or his sense of humor? How about his knowledge of the job that he does or the way he manages people in the workplace? Perhaps you respect him for the way he tends to things around your home like the yard, the cars, or the necessary repairs. Take a lesson from Otis Redding and Aretha Franklin: let him know. Sock it to him. In the process, you'll notice an amazing thing. Your ability to love him will increase as well.

Write down a characteristic of your partner that inspires your respect.

Have I Told You Lately?

"Do you miss me?" I asked Lori over the phone while out of town.

"Yeah, I miss ya," she said.

I was underwhelmed by her tone of voice and looking for a bit more.

"No, do you *miss* me?"

"Yeah, I miss ya," she repeated.

Now I felt let down by her lack of enthusiasm. I could tell something was up. I planned to talk with her once I got back in town. My first night home, before we could talk, I overheard her on the phone in another room. She was telling her best friend, "Lately I feel more like a single mom. Jud is just gone all the time." My heart sank through the floor.

I knew I had been pushing too hard at work, but I was oblivious to what my wife had been feeling. As soon as she was off the phone, I sat down with her to talk. "Even when you're home, you're mentally checked out," she explained. "Right now, it does not feel any different for me whether you are in town or not."

She was right, and I needed to hear it. I had to be honest with myself and with her. So we looked at our relationship, and I began the difficult process of restructuring my life. Lori receives love through quality time, so I've got to be there with all my faculties intact. We have adjusted our lives, and it has made a tremendous difference.

Relationships drift when you set them on autopilot. Though Van Morrison wrote "Have I Told You Lately?" Rod Stewart recorded it for his wife, Rachel Hunter. Yet after nine years of marriage, Rachel divorced him and was later reported to have said he "got boring."[8] Relational drift can happen to anyone, which is why communicating love is so important.

Solomon and the Shulammite knew how to communicate love to one another. In the Song, we can hear what was important to this wife. She says, "Dark am I, yet lovely, O daughters of Jerusalem, dark like the tents of Kedar, like the tent curtains of Solomon. Do not stare at me because I am dark, because I am darkened by the sun. My mother's sons were angry with me and made me take care of the vineyards; my own vineyard I have neglected" (1:5, 6).

Today people go to great lengths to be tan, using tanning lotions and salons. Being tan is seen as a desirable feature. But in Solomon's time having a tan showed that you were a laborer who worked in the fields. So his bride says, "Don't look down on me because of my tan. Don't despise me because I'm of lower social standing than you." Her tan isn't something she likes about herself.

We all have things that we don't like about ourselves. For example, the top of my right ear has ridges on it. It feels like someone cut my ear with craft scissors. I call it my Spock ear. You could stand two feet from me and look at my ear without noticing it; but I know it is there, and I have a complex about it. For others, the problem is not their ears, but their feet or their hips or their faces. There are things we just don't like about ourselves. And for the Shulammite, it is her tan.

What is Solomon's response? Through the course of the Song, he communicates love to her in a way that elevates her self-image. Early on she expresses self-doubt, but as the Song continues, we see that she finds more confidence. By 8:7 she says she is more valuable to Solomon than all of his wealth. In 8:10-12 she says she can make him content and that she believes she's worth more to him than all of his vineyards. Her self-worth has been transformed from being very low to seeing herself as the most valuable thing in her mate's world.

How does this transformation occur? Solomon effectively communicates love to her so that she understands it, receives it, and owns it. He refers to her as "my darling" (1:9). The phrase "my darling" can be literally translated "my female friend." Solomon and the woman had developed a friendship. Research shows that friendship is what both men and women want from a relationship. Friendship sets the course for everything else. A couple may bicker or argue, but their friendship keeps these arguments from rocking their relationship. The primary thing that holds couples together is not conflict resolution techniques, but a friendship that overcomes significant differences.

RELATIONSHIPS DRIFT WHEN YOU SET THEM ON AUTOPILOT.

So let's take a little quiz: Do you know your spouse's hopes and dreams? Can you describe who he or she is frustrated with right now? Do you know his or her biggest fear? Too often people live together and yet know little about each other. I've been surprised at how many married people know little about the inner world of their spouses. Get to know your spouse again and cultivate your friendship.

"I liken you, my darling," says Solomon, "to a mare harnessed to one of the chariots of Pharaoh" (1:9). Whoa! What's that all about? You probably don't want to compare your wife to a harnessed mare. Just trust me on that one!

Here's the significance in Solomon's culture: Military powers harnessed stallions, not mares, to their chariots. When the stallions were about to charge into battle with all the soldiers on chariots, the opposing side could bring out mares in heat. The stallions would then lose focus as their attention suddenly shifted from the battlefield to the mares. The result was chaos.

So Solomon implies that when his wife walks into the room, all his attention shifts to her. Everything stops. She is his greatest distraction, the apple of his eye. There is no one like her in his world. With these words he is communicating love to her.

"Your cheeks are beautiful with earrings, your neck with strings of jewels," says Solomon. "We will make you earrings of gold, studded with silver" (1:10, 11). Jewelry complements her beauty, and he knows she loves it. (Ladies, if you are looking for a biblical proof text for men to buy you jewelry—this is it!)

IT'S THE LITTLE THINGS THAT ADD UP.

Men may be tempted to read this and think, *That's it, I'll buy her a diamond and be covered for six months.* Men tend to think they get big points for big gifts. We think buying our wives rings or necklaces will put us in good standing for the long haul. But men and women keep score differently. Some women may enjoy bigger gifts, but that doesn't get the men off the hook. Guys should still open doors, send cards, and give compliments. It's the little things that add up. But whether the gift is flowers or a diamond, it still counts as only one point to a woman. (Although my wife insists a vacation to Hawaii would be worth a couple points!)

Solomon learned to communicate love in a way his partner could receive it. He was generous with gifts, but he also communicated love to her verbally. As a result, her self-image flourished and came to match his loving words. For both men and women, it is crucial that love is communicated in a way our partners will best receive it.

Gary Chapman has popularized the idea of love languages in his book *The Five Love Languages*. He lists as the primary ways people receive love: quality time, words of affirmation, gifts, acts of service, and physical touch.[9] Often we show love to our spouses in *our* love languages, not *theirs*. Early in my marriage, if I really wanted to go all out for my wife, I would clean the house. I'd go nuts getting everything perfect. When my wife came home, I greeted her at the door proclaiming the cleanliness of our house. I extolled the amazing dust-free environment she entered. I wanted her to do cartwheels or backflips, or throw herself into my arms in ecstasy.

"Looks good," she would say. "Can I tell you about my day?"

I would stand there at the door feeling dejected and thinking, *"Looks good." Is that all I get for slaving away here all day?!*

It took two years for me to realize *I* wanted the house clean, not my wife. She is a people person who remains laid-back about the house. I was trying to communicate love to her in my love language, which is acts of service, instead of in hers.

What makes Lori feel loved is quality time. When I talk to her for an hour, I communicate a great deal of love. To meet Lori's needs, I sit down and communicate with her. She in turn knocks herself out on the house because she realizes how important that is to me.

Write down the top five things that cause you to feel loved, and share them with your partner. You may be surprised. This one simple action can take years off learning how to communicate love to your spouse. It will also ensure you are missed when you leave town!

Share with your mate your list of what causes you to feel loved.

Girls Just Want to Have Fun

It was a hot Texas day I will never forget. With each passing moment my expectations rose. Finally, as six o'clock came, I pulled up in Lori's driveway and made my way to the door. We smiled for a photo her parents insisted on and headed out for what she thought was a normal date. My plan was to take her for a romantic meal and then to a park, where I would ask her to marry me.

Everything went perfectly. We arrived at the restaurant on the top floor of the tallest building in our city, and took our places for dinner. During the meal I casually looked out the window and saw that it was raining—not the sprinkling kind of rain, drenching rain. My plan washed away before my eyes.

I panicked.

Remaining calm and cool on the outside, I desperately pieced together plan B on the inside. I had no choice but to propose in the restaurant. My only problem: the ring was several stories below, in my car. I excused myself and took the elevator to the bottom floor. After making the mad dash to the car for the ring, I was completely soaked.

"Where have you been?" Lori asked, as I sat back down at the table.

"I ran down to the car."

"Why?"

Suddenly all my romantic charm came out in one classic guy response: "Uh, my nose has been really stopped up, and I needed to get my nasal spray." (*Nasal spray!* What was I thinking?! Little did she know that, being male, I made these kinds of "perfect moment" sayings all the time.)

"That's funny," she said. "I have your nasal spray right here in my purse."

I was caught. Busted. I thought, *Should I take the nasal spray and use it? No. That would be wrong.*

Instead, I took her hands in mine and quoted a passage from the book of Ruth: "Don't urge me to leave you or to turn back from you. Where you go I will go, and where you stay I will stay. Your people will be my people and your God my God. Where you die I will die, and there I will be buried" (Ruth 1:16, 17).

Then I walked around the table, dropped to my knee, and asked, "Will you be my date for life? Will you marry me?" In that moment there was only one word I wanted to hear—yes. After Lori said that word, I can't remember much else.

But here is the unfortunate part of the story. For me and many guys, the most creative date we've ever planned was the night of our proposal or our honeymoon. Cyndi Lauper's tune "Girls Just Want to Have Fun" plays in the movie *Clueless*, which is exactly what men can be in the area of dating. Guys are pursuers by nature. We go after a prize. We're engaged in the dating process until we win her heart and she accepts the ring. The prize is won! Our tendency is then to move on to the next challenge.

But after we are married, we can't stop pursuing and dating our mates. They still need to be pursued. I can't fall back on the night I asked Lori to marry me years ago. It's absolutely critical that I continue to creatively date my wife.

The related principle we see in the Song of Solomon is simply this: have an awesome time. The Shulammite says, "Tell me, you whom I love, where you graze your flock and where you rest your sheep at midday" (1:7). It's as if she's saying, "Let's have a little lunch date. Tell me where you are going to be and we'll get together." Then she says, "Why should I be like a veiled woman beside the flocks of your friends?" (1:7). In other words, "Tell me where you are going to be for lunch, or I might just go to lunch with one of your friends instead. Let's set something up."

CYNDI LAUPER'S TUNE "GIRLS JUST WANT TO HAVE FUN" PLAYS IN THE MOVIE CLUELESS, WHICH IS EXACTLY WHAT MEN CAN BE IN THE AREA OF DATING.

The friends respond by playfully refusing to tell her where he'll be. "If you do not know, most beautiful of women, follow the tracks of the sheep and graze your young goats by the tents of the shepherds" (1:8). They're saying, "Go and find him. You chase him a little bit!"

What are Solomon and the Shulammite doing? They are planning a rendezvous, and you can tell they have a great time doing it. They are setting aside this time to be together.

The greatest threat to our marriages and families today is not financial problems, or infidelity, or the state of the Union. The greatest threat is busyness. We are doing so much, there is no margin in which to cultivate relationships.

Lori and I set time weeks in advance to connect and have fun. We lock these times in as an immovable appointment with each other. It's important that we go out and have a good time not only for us, but for our kids. They need to see that we value each other in that way. Some couples have thrived in marriages for decades without ever going on a date, but they learned how to cultivate the relationship their own way. For Lori and me, the date night works.

One of the major barriers in maintaining a date night is children. Sometimes you can't find the time or you can't bear to part with them. Other times you feel that you can't justify the babysitting costs. Yet we are better parents, with healthier homes, when we as couples take time to be alone together on a regular basis. Kids sense when Mom and Dad's relationship is thriving, and when it is not. They pick up on these things more than we give them credit for.

THE GREATEST THREAT TO OUR MARRIAGES AND FAMILIES TODAY IS NOT FINANCIAL PROBLEMS, OR INFIDELITY, OR THE STATE OF THE UNION. THE GREATEST THREAT IS BUSYNESS.

One of the greatest gifts you can give your children is to exemplify the kind of marriage you would like them to have in the future. They are likely to follow and repeat what they see in their parents. So schedule your date night! If you can't bear to part with the children, do it in small steps. They will probably have fun being with someone other than Mom or Dad. If you can't afford a sitter, make arrangements with a family member or trade babysitting time with a trusted friend who also needs to get out. Or just give my wife, Lori, a call. She loves to watch kids. Just kidding! Don't do that, or I may be bunking on the couch for a while.

What did you do together before marriage? How did you spend your time together? Did you play tennis or go bowling? Did you take walks in the park or at the mall? Did you take long drives and bring a picnic? Think about those things that brought joy to you when dating and do those things all over again—or do them in a new way. You might take turns on your date night, first doing something that one of you likes, and then something the other chooses. Both girls and guys want to have fun, so don't stop dating!

Stop right now and schedule a date night on the calendar.

Tell Her About It

When Billy Joel's "Tell Her About It" fills the air at the grocery store as I shop, it stays with me all day. I hum it, tap my feet to it, lip-synch it, and eventually drive everyone around me nuts. No matter how much I try to turn it off, Billy keeps telling her about it in my head. But it is a message I need to hear.

Studies show the average woman speaks thousands more words a day than the average guy. I've seen this play out in my family. At eighteen months old my daughter walked through our house imitating her mother. She could not yet talk at the time, but that didn't hold her back. She held the phone to her ear and said "Hello, dabba dabba da, dabba dabba da" into a dead receiver. Periodically she'd say "bye-bye," lower the phone for three seconds, and then repeat the process. She talked more on the phone—before she could speak words—than many adult males do!

Many women think their relationships are going great when they and their partners are talking a lot. Many guys think their relationships are going great when they are *not* talking a lot. Men and women see things from different perspectives. Picture, if you dare, a bachelor's bathroom. He's got six items—shaving cream, a razor, toothpaste, a toothbrush, a bar of soap, and a towel he ripped off from the Holiday Inn. Now picture a bachelorette's bathroom. She has 237 items, most of which are completely foreign to guys. Women are more complex than men in a lot of ways. All of these differences come out in communication.

She says, "We never talk."

He takes her literally and replies, "We talk all the time. We talked last night. What more do you want?"

She doesn't literally mean they never talk. She means, "I have a huge need for you to listen to me and connect with me in a deep way. I don't feel like we have connected in a while, and you don't seem interested. Would you please sit down with me and communicate?"

Women often make categorical statements using *never* and *always*, but they are trying to get to something deeper than the literal words. Categorical statements express their frustrations, yet men tend to hear things literally.

The first two chapters of the Song of Solomon are great examples of communication between a husband and a wife. In these verses we see that they have learned to listen and understand one another as much as possible. Solomon says, "How beautiful you are, my darling! Oh, how beautiful! Your eyes are doves" (1:15). In the ancient world, eyes were seen as an indicator of personality. We still say that eyes are the windows to the soul. Solomon is saying, "You are beautiful inside and out." Ladies need to hear that again and again.

SHE SAYS, "WE NEVER TALK."

The Shulammite responds, "How handsome you are, my lover! Oh, how charming! And our bed is verdant" (1:16). He expresses affection and touches her mind and emotions. Feeling loved and cared for, she responds by saying how handsome he is and how their bed is verdant, or lush. They are meeting each other's needs.

If you're going to communicate, listening must be involved. This is often a challenge for guys who fashion themselves after Bob Vila—

Mr. Fix-it. Many husbands want to be the guy who can "use an Allen wrench in twenty-seven different ways" (as advertised on The Learning Channel). They need to "fix it" around the house, "fix it" at the office, and they also want to "fix it" in their relationships.

However, when a wife approaches her husband to talk about a problem or upsetting situation, she is rarely seeking advice. What she needs is someone to listen—not to come up with a solution, not even to give a deep diagnostic of what's going on. She wants him to listen. The point of communication is communication. The goal of communication is communication.

Sometimes a woman comes home and unloads her emotions on her husband. He, being literal and wanting to fix it, becomes overwhelmed. He's thinking, *Our family is cracking up; we're falling apart. How am I going to keep all this together? How can I help my wife get a grip?*

Before the conversation, she feels stressed and overwhelmed. After the conversation, she feels relieved because she got the problem off her chest. Just in the act of communication, she has unloaded and feels better. Now *he* feels burdened. Yet often the best a guy can do is just listen and let go.

In the Song the woman says, "I am a rose of Sharon, a lily of the valleys" (2:1). Now you may think, *Wow, she thinks she's all that.* But let's look at the context. There are a million lilies on the plains of Sharon. She's really saying, "I'm one among many. I'm just like one rose of Sharon or a lily of the valley. I'm just a normal gal."

Do you know what she's doing with these words? She's fishing for a compliment. It's like the old "Do I look fat in these jeans?" question. It isn't about the jeans.

Solomon picks up on this, and he responds, "Like a lily among thorns is my darling among the maidens." In other words, "You are one in a million. There is no one else like you." Nice job, Solomon.

He dialed in and he communicated right back. He listened, not just to what she said but also to what she meant.

She replies, "Like an apple tree among the trees of the forest is my lover among the young men" (2:3). There are not a lot of apple trees in the forest. She's responding with her own analogy to declare that he also is special and unique.

We're getting a beautiful picture of a married couple reflecting on their relationship, and it's awesome! Too many conversations between married couples center on the trivial things of life—"Pick your boxers up off the floor!" "When are you going to drop off the kid?" "You spent *how* much money?" But we have to go deeper in our communication. And we need to send more positive verbal messages.

INVEST IN YOUR RELATIONSHIP BY MAKING SMALL AND FREQUENT DEPOSITS, EXPRESSING YOUR LOVE TO HER EVERY DAY.

Dr. Gottman's research revealed that the one determining factor in a relationship's survival is what he calls the magic ratio. Couples who remained together had five affirming comments for every negative one in their dialogue.[10] A couple might yell and scream when they fight, and our tendency would be to think they aren't going to make it. But in reality they may be very satisfied with their relationship. They have passionate disagreements, but they also have passionate reunions. They can thrive because they maintain the magic ratio of positive comments to negative ones.

Among the positive comments that a guy can make is a particularly important one: tell your wife you love her. Tell her in the way you look at her and in the way you treat her. Tell her in front of her friends. Tell her you love her hair and the way she looks. Tell her she is your one in a million. She'll love and respect you all the more for it. Invest in your relationship by making small and frequent deposits, expressing your love to her every day. The time is now. May Billy Joel's tune get stuck in your mind until you "tell her about it."

Write down a couple things you love about your spouse and tell him or her about them.

PLAYLIST No. 2

THRIVING AFTER "I DO"

Chapel of Love

Ever sung the wrong words to a song? It can be incredibly embarrassing. The Dixie Cups' "Chapel of Love" is one of the most recognizable tunes ever, but I read of one woman who misunderstood the words. On a first date she sang, "Goin' to the chuck hole, and we're going to get married. . . . Goin' to the chuck hole of love." She couldn't figure out why her date looked at her like she was nuts!

I've seen some "chuck hole" moments at weddings, like the bride who walked down the aisle as the Darth Vader theme music from *Star Wars* blared, compliments of the groom. Funny, but tough on the honeymoon! I've seen a Disney wedding with *Beauty and the Beast* special music. Great for the bride, but I wonder what the groom thought? I've heard a bride sing to her groom in the absolute worst voice a human can have. He looked beet red and totally embarrassed. Love is not blind (or deaf!) to everything. However, no matter how bumpy the weddings get, there is always a celebration of two people uniting in love.

The first two chapters of the Song contained the couple's dialogue about their passion and the amazing nature of love. But in 3:6, the tone changes. The Shulammite describes her wedding day, the day she had thought about for her entire life.

Isn't that how girls are? Little girls play wedding while little boys kill each other with swords. Later, girls peruse bridal magazines through high school and college. Even without any dating prospects, they design gowns, choose colors, and plan the place and time of year for the wedding. It will all be perfect. They should know. They've dreamed of walking down the aisle their whole lives.

IT WILL ALL BE PERFECT. THEY SHOULD KNOW. THEY'VE DREAMED OF WALKING DOWN THE AISLE THEIR WHOLE LIVES.

In the Song of Solomon, the Shulammite remembers: "Who is this coming up from the desert like a column of smoke, perfumed with myrrh and incense made from all the spices of the merchant? Look! It is Solomon's carriage." (3:6, 7). It is their wedding day, and the groom is making his entry. He is glorious in royal colors, coming in his carriage to pick up his bride.

Weddings in that culture were quite different from what we experience. Today the wedding is about the bride. When I facilitate wedding rehearsals, I say to the wedding party, "Keep your eyes on the bride. Never look away from the bride. If the bride runs out the back door, watch her go and smile like we planned it." After the wedding people say, "She looked amazing! She was stunning." Nobody says much of anything about the groom; it is the bride's day.

In ancient Israel, people focused on the groom. All eyes were fixed on him. Here the woman in the Song is remembering how amazing it was to see Solomon coming in his royal carriage. In that culture the groom would go to the bride's house in a processional. From there the processional went to the groom's father's for the marriage feast. At the end of the feast, the father of the bride presented a marriage agreement or covenant to the bride and groom to sign. The bride's father would also sign it, and then the price for the bride was paid. This was the last step in courtship. Then the couple was officially united.

Once their union was official, they went off for some private time to consummate the marriage physically. After that, everyone celebrated the wedding. I mean, *really* celebrated the wedding. The party might go on for a week or two! They took marriage and the celebration of it seriously.

God designed marriage for the good of mankind. We were created to exist in the context of relationships. Think of Adam in the Garden of Eden. He had direct access to God. He had never sinned. He experienced paradise in the way God intended. The guy had no bills, no taxes, and no worries. Yet it was not enough. God looked at Adam's situation and said, "It is not good for the man to be alone. I will make a helper suitable for him" (Genesis 2:18). The implications here are astounding. People often talk of just needing God in their life. But Adam had God, and it was "not good" that he was alone. He needed others and so do we. So God formed the woman from the side of man.

The first time Adam laid eyes on Eve, he felt blown away. Adam broke into verse: "This is now bone of my bones and flesh of my flesh; she shall be called 'woman,' for she was taken out of man" (Genesis 2:23). Her beauty moved him. It is the first time we see poetry in the Bible. The woman is literally the bone and flesh of Adam; thus, when God unites a man and a wife he is fusing them together as one flesh.

I've been privileged to stand at the altar and look into the eyes of couples in love. You can see the hope and anticipation they have for their marriage. So it's heartbreaking to see some of them back in my office a few years later for pastoral counseling. Now I see heartache and pain. Sadly, by the time they land in a pastor's office, the relationship has gone through so much damage it's almost irreparable.

We can keep ourselves from reaching that point by paying attention to our marriages. Like the Shulammite, we can remember the day of our vows and reflect on what they mean. Marriage is a covenant relationship in which two people commit themselves to one another. Genesis 2:24 says, "For this reason a man will leave his father and mother and be united to his wife, and they will become one flesh." There is a leaving aspect in marriage, a loosening of the parent-child relationship. And there is a uniting aspect as two people share their lives. The two become one flesh, which refers not only to the physical consummation of marriage but also to the spiritual union. Marriage is more than a piece of paper—it's a promise between two people and God. Marriage constitutes a devotion to stick with a person through good times and bad, thick and thin, wealth and poverty.

MARRIAGE IS MORE THAN A PIECE OF PAPER—IT'S A PROMISE BETWEEN TWO PEOPLE AND GOD.

In this section, we'll go back to the chapel and consider how we can thrive after we say "I do," in spite of the "chuck holes" along the journey. We'll look at practical ways to fulfill the vows we took—to have and to hold our spouses in sickness and in health, in prosperity and in need, and till death do us part. And we'll consider how Solomon's wedding can inspire us to meet each other's needs. So let's return to the "Chapel of Love."

Take a few minutes, look at your wedding ring, and reminisce about the commitment you made.

I Only Have Eyes for You

For years after our marriage, on our anniversary Lori "forced" me to watch cheap video footage of our wedding. After five years I developed a horrible attitude about watching it. Yet each time I viewed myself waiting for her to come down the aisle, I remembered that moment. I had stood there thinking, *Wow! I got the best end of this deal! I can't believe she really is marrying me.* And now as I watched that scene again, I changed my attitude. Attitude has more to do with the success or failure of a marriage than circumstances, money, sex, or children do. And, thankfully, we can choose our attitude.

In the Song of Solomon, the Shulammite chooses a great attitude toward Solomon. She reflects on her wedding day, as if watching the video of the ceremony again: "Who is this coming up from the desert like a column of smoke," she says, "perfumed with myrrh and incense made from all the spices of the merchant?" (3:6).

In the early chapters of Exodus, God led the people of Israel with a pillar of cloud during the day and a pillar of fire by night. This became significant history in their culture. They related the story down through generations. According to some commentators, the bride is saying, "Solomon, I see you coming as if led by God himself to take me in this processional to be your wife. You are the one and only person for me."

She sees God's involvement in bringing the two of them together. He is leading them, just as he led Israel through the wilderness.

When we struggle in our marriages, we could be tempted to think, *Maybe he wasn't the person God wanted me to be with.* Or *Maybe she isn't the one for me.* We may rationalize that if we were with the person God wanted for us, this union would be easy. *If this person were my soul mate, everything would be smooth and effortless.* Some believe in a romantic concept that there is only one soul mate out there for every person. If we just find that one individual, then we will be happy.

Let's take this thinking to its logical conclusion. If you think there is only one person you are meant to marry and that you married the wrong person, then the person who was supposed to marry your spouse also married the wrong person. This means the person who was supposed to marry the person who married your spouse also married the wrong person. If you trace it back logically, the entire human race married the wrong person just because one person did.

So either we get all six billion people on earth together for a cosmic relational shuffle, or we change our thinking about the idea of a soul mate. How we view this is important because it affects our attitudes. The truth is, before we get married there are several people we *could* marry. Before marriage, we should pray regularly, date wisely, and invest some time in premarital counseling. The more groundwork we do up front, the better the foundation we lay for our relationships. That's the perspective *before* marriage.

After marriage, our husbands or wives are our soul mates, the only ones for us. That doesn't mean our relationships will be easy. Marriage may still be hard; it will take work, and we will experience tension. But here's why it is so important to view your spouse as your one and only: How we think determines how we act, which determines how we feel. If you start letting your mind go to a place where you say "I'm not sure

God wanted us together; I don't know if he or she is the one," then you open yourself up to asking, "Why try to make it work?"

Now let's take it from the opposite angle. If you start telling yourself "Yes, this relationship is hard right now, but God brought us together; how can we work though our difficulties?" that puts you in a whole different state of mind. Rather than thinking of a way *out*, you focus on a way *forward*. You move toward a solution that starts with your attitude.

EITHER WE GET ALL SIX BILLION PEOPLE ON EARTH TOGETHER FOR A COSMIC RELATIONAL SHUFFLE, OR WE CHANGE OUR THINKING ABOUT THE IDEA OF A SOUL MATE.

We can learn from the Shulammite as she reflects on her wedding day. She hangs on to the fact that God brought her and her mate together. They continually view one another as the only one for them in passages such as "My lover is mine and I am his" (2:16), and "I belong to my lover, and his desire is for me" (7:10).

Having this attitude toward one another is a choice they made that changed how they acted and felt toward each other. But each day we choose how we will view our spouses.

In Marcus Buckingham's book *The One Thing You Need to Know*, he cites a fascinating study on the power of attitude in marriage. Buckingham writes of Dr. Sandra Murray, a professor at SUNY Buffalo, and her team, who asked 105 couples to rate the qualities of their partners and then rate the overall satisfaction in the relationship. These couples had been together on average for 10.9 years. Common sense would say that if a husband rated his wife highly in one quality, such as "warm and patient," and the wife rated herself similarly in both her strengths and weaknesses, then they would have a happy marriage.

After all, they have a realistic, matching perspective of each other. Yet that is not what the research showed. Husbands and wives whose ratings matched were no more or less likely to be satisfied.

Only one primary pattern emerged in their research. In the happiest couples, the husband consistently rated his wife higher than she rated herself in every category. The husband remained somewhat blind to her weaknesses. He attributed positive qualities to her that she did not attribute to herself.

The skeptic asks, "What happens over time when she inevitably disappoints him?" The research team had similar questions, so they followed these couples for several years. In the end, the couples whose husbands rated their wives higher in every category had *more* satisfaction with the relationship after several years, not less. There was less conflict, doubt, and tension, along with growing satisfaction.

Buckingham boils down the meaning of this research. "The one thing you need to know about happy marriage: Find the most generous explanation for each other's behavior and believe it. . . . When you notice a flaw, recast it in your mind as an aspect of strength. Thus 'She's not narrow-minded, she's focused.'"[11] The research shows that our attitudes toward our spouses will make or break the relationship.

"THE ONE THING YOU NEED TO KNOW ABOUT HAPPY MARRIAGE: FIND THE MOST GENEROUS EXPLANATION FOR EACH OTHER'S BEHAVIOR AND BELIEVE IT."

There is a sense in all this that may make you wonder if you are playing mind games. But all you are really doing is keeping your attitude in check. When you change your attitude and focus on your spouse's strengths, it changes how you feel toward him or her. When you reflect on your relationship and realize God allowed you to come together, you are inspired to trust him in your marriage.

The Shulammite sees her groom coming out of the wilderness as if led by God himself. The commitment of marriage is a commitment of three, not two. It is you, your spouse, *and* God. He is at work in human relationships. This means you do not have to face the challenges alone. You do not have to go through the vicious cycles of arguing alone. If you struggle with commitment, bring God into the middle of the struggle. If you fight over money, bring God into the middle of your finances. If communication breaks down, bring God into the middle of the breakdown. By focusing on your attitude toward your spouse, you can experience a healthy perspective on your relationship. Quit murmuring to yourself about where he or she is lacking, and talk about the strengths. Give yourself an attitude adjustment toward your one and only. The good news is, you don't have to watch cheap video footage of your wedding ceremony for that!

Focus on all your spouse is, rather than on what he or she is not.

Where Is the Love?

The first time I heard the Black Eyed Peas' song "Where Is the Love?" I was riding in the car with my friend Mike. I was blown away by this post-9/11 anthem for peace and love in the world. While I love the song's message, I felt frustrated at my failures to show love to my own spouse, much less the world. Sometimes the hardest people to consistently love are the ones closest to you.

The *Saturday Evening Post* ran an article titled "The Seven Ages of the Married Cold," which chronicled a husband's treatment of his wife in seven years of marriage.

> The first year: "Sugar dumpling, I'm worried about my baby girl. You've got a bad sniffle, and there's no telling about these things with all this strep around. I'm putting you in the hospital this afternoon for a general checkup and a good rest. I know the food's lousy, but I'll bring your meals in from Rossini's. I've already got it arranged with the floor superintendent."
>
> The second year: "Listen, darling, I don't like the sound of that cough. I've called Doc Miller to rush over here. Now, you go to bed like a good girl, please? . . ."
>
> The third year: "Maybe you'd better lie down, honey; nothing like a little rest when you're feeling punk. I'll bring you something to eat. Have we got any soup?"

The fourth year: "Look, dear, be sensible. After you feed the kids and get the dishes washed, you'd better hit the sack."

The fifth year: "Why don't you get yourself a couple of aspirin?"

The sixth year: "Why don't you gargle or something, rather than sitting around barking like a seal!"

The seventh year: "For Pete's sake, stop sneezing! What are you trying to do, give me pneumonia?"[12]

Where is the love? We can travel a long way from the concern of the honeymoon phase. This is why I'm impressed by the tone of the Song of Solomon as the couple remains passionate about one another. They maintain a closeness that is both inspiring and humbling. They learned to meet one another's needs, even after they said "I do."

In modern weddings we take one another "to have and to hold." The terms point back to the biblical account of marriage in which God says the couple will be "united" together. The Hebrew word implies holding or clinging to one another. We see Solomon and the Shulammite embracing one another physically. The book opens with her declaring, "Let him kiss me with the kisses of his mouth" (1:2). Later we read: "His left arm is under my head, and his right arm embraces me" (2:6).

Physical closeness is important, but so is emotional closeness. In the Song of Solomon, he writes that she is like a "dove in the clefts of the rock, in the hiding places on the mountainside" (2:14). As the dove withdraws and hides in the clefts, so the woman has withdrawn to emotional hiding places. She may be struggling with previous relational baggage or simply the fear of being vulnerable. He says, "Show me your face" (v. 14), which literally means her "presence." He longs for her to be real and open with him as a person. "Let me hear your voice," he says, "for your voice is sweet, and your face is lovely" (v. 14). He calls on her to drop her guard and draw near to him emotionally. And she does.

PHYSICAL CLOSENESS IS IMPORTANT, BUT SO IS EMOTIONAL CLOSENESS.

Both having and holding are important actions in a relationship. But men and women, having different needs, generally have different perspectives of what they entail. For example, some men are energized from what I call proximity time. This is time just spent in proximity to one another, in the same room. It doesn't have to involve any activity done together, though you could be watching a movie or having a meal. But sometimes I'll call my wife to come and sit with me for no reason, just to have her by my side. I might be reading a book or paying the bills. She may be thinking, *He's got something on his mind or he wouldn't have asked me to come in here.* But do you know what I'm thinking about? Absolutely nothing. I don't want to talk about anything. I'm just reading a book, and I like my wife to be close to me. This kind of side-by-side time is important for some men. For him, "to have and to hold" can simply involve her presence.

Women have a significant need for closeness in the relationship, but it often plays out differently. For her, closeness is often connected to conversation. It is so important to her that he open up about his feelings and what is going on inside. Also, physical contact that is not leading to something else is meaningful. We say to others "Let's keep in touch," but we need to keep "in touch" literally in our relationships. Just hold her hand or give her a hug. All these little things communicate love.

When it comes to maintaining closeness in a relationship, we should be careful about the connection between our actions and feelings. Too often we base our actions solely on our feelings, but feelings are fickle. A spouse may withdraw emotionally or physically from his or her partner, saying "I'm just not *feeling* it right now." Instead of letting your feelings drive your actions, I propose you do the opposite. Reverse the cycle and allow your actions to shape your feelings. Go back to the moment you exchanged vows. Return to the days of dating your spouse, when you couldn't wait to see that person again. What did you do for her when you felt love and excitement? What did you do for him? Start doing those things again.

YOUR VOWS DIDN'T SAY ANYTHING ABOUT WHETHER OR NOT YOU FELT LIKE IT.

Now that may seem hypocritical. "I don't feel like I love him," you say, "and you want me to tell him I love him and do what we used to do?" Yes! It's not being hypocritical. If you are struggling and feeling tension in your marriage, then doing something positive about it honors the marriage vows you took. Your vows didn't say anything about whether or not you felt like it. The vows said, "I take you to be my lawfully wedded wife (or husband)." So take action and get involved in your relationship. John writes, "No one has ever seen God; but if we love one another, God lives in us and his love is made complete in us"(1 John 4:12). God's love is made complete as we do the actions of love. Act like you are in love, and eventually you may *feel* like you are in love.

> For the next month, act toward your spouse like you used to do when you were in the honeymoon phase.

Dedicated to the One I Love

Years ago I worked at a place that threw a huge bash billed as Woodstock II. In reality, it wasn't huge; it was held at a cheesy water park in Albuquerque, New Mexico, and it was years before the real Woodstock II. The only band I remember was The Mamas and the Papas, although I felt a little confused because it was more like the daughters and their papas. I don't recall much of their set because I ran one of the spotlights, but I do remember the guy barking in my headset to "keep the spotlight on the bass player!" After the show I spent hours cleaning up all kinds of paraphernalia from those who still thought it was 1969 in the '80s. One of the tunes they played was "Dedicated to the One I Love," a song the bass player performed very well—and with good spotlighting. The best marriages put a spotlight on serious dedication between a man and woman.

When I dated Lori she periodically threw out questions to check my dedication.

"Would you love me if I gained a hundred pounds?" she'd ask.

"Would you love me if I had a debilitating disease?"

"Would you love me if I became an invalid?"

She fished around to see if I would love her unconditionally. Ever asked similar questions? They get to the heart of a person's need for security, which is a huge thing in every marriage.

As the Shulammite reflects on her wedding day, she recalls the strength and security she found in Solomon. She writes, "Look! It is Solomon's carriage, escorted by sixty warriors, the noblest of Israel, all of them wearing the sword, all experienced in battle, each with his sword at his side, prepared for the terrors of the night" (3:7, 8).

"WOULD YOU LOVE ME IF I GAINED A HUNDRED POUNDS?"

As Solomon came to pick her up in the processional, his carriage was an elaborate portable bed. He came with sixty warriors, experienced in battle. There was no threat they could not handle. This was twice the number of mighty men that would accompany the great King David in battle. The message was clear—he would protect her.

Earlier in the Song of Solomon she writes of feeling completely secure in his presence: "I delight to sit in his shade, and his fruit is sweet to my taste. He has taken me to the banquet hall, and his banner over me is love" (2:3, 4). Sitting in his shade is a reference to the security she feels with him. His presence offers a shield from the world and refreshment for her soul. She says that his "banner" over her is love, which can be translated as his "gaze" or "look" over her is love. Just by his look she knows his intentions are for love. The security she feels with him inspires her to respond in a physically intimate way.

When we stand at the altar and vow to a marriage "in sickness and in health," we make promises about dedication and security. We don't have to show up at a wedding like Solomon, with sixty mighty men trained in battle, to communicate security. There are some very simple things we can do to help each other feel secure in our relationships. In fact, many say the little things are more important than big things when it comes to making them feel secure.

One significant way I have learned to communicate dedication is to come home on time. I'm never late for work-related appointments because I feel that is disrespectful. Yet when it came to being home on time, I was much more lax. I would say I'd be home at 6:30 PM and then roll in at 7:00 or 7:30 PM. This went on all the time, and I never thought much about it. Finally, my wife pointed out this disparity. She communicated that it made her feel less valuable and less important than all the other things I made sure I was on time for. Once I realized how she felt, I made an effort to change how I structured my life. So now, I honor the time I say I'll be home. When I walk in on time, it's a good thing for everyone.

Another area in which we can help our spouses feel secure is in how we talk about the opposite sex. When a guy sits with his wife and a beautiful woman passes by, it is not smart to say, "Wow! Now that girl is beautiful! Why don't you look more like that?" You don't want to go there! Nor is it helpful for women to comment in front of their husbands about how good-looking another guy is.

We often do these things in a teasing and lighthearted way, but it sends signals to our partners. Each comment can make them feel a little more insecure about who they are. Sometimes when we're watching a movie, Lori asks, "Do you think she is pretty?"

I respond, "Who? Catherine Zeta-Jones? Not as pretty as you, dear." I don't even go there. Images of beautiful people fill our magazine racks. Their photos are treated and airbrushed; yet they look so real. Many of us wrestle with deep insecurities about appearance. So when we make comments about others to our spouses, they may think, *I could never look like that. That's what my spouse likes and it's not me. I'll never be so thin or tan or beautiful.* Do yourself and your spouse a big favor. Stay away from comments about the opposite sex that can foster insecurity.

We can also increase security in our relationships by how we interact with the opposite sex. As a pastor, I made a decision to never counsel a woman alone. I always have someone else in the room. One of the reasons for this is to honor my wife. I want her and everyone else to know that she's the most important person in my life. I also avoid going out for a meal with another woman alone. I'm not saying it's always wrong, or that we need to be legalistic here, but we should be cautious of those situations and aware of how our partners feel about them. Consistently spending one-on-one time with a member of the opposite sex may cause feelings of jealousy and insecurity in one's spouse.

WE DON'T HAVE TO SHOW UP AT A WEDDING LIKE SOLOMON, WITH SIXTY MIGHTY MEN TRAINED IN BATTLE, TO COMMUNICATE SECURITY.

I've heard people argue that it is not fair for their spouses to get upset when they spend time with an ex-girlfriend or an ex-boyfriend. For example, she asks him to stop meeting with this ex-girlfriend for lunch. He's says, "I love you. We're married. She's just my friend." And he feels this request is too much. Yet when we exchange vows we agree to honor, love, and support our spouses more than anyone else. It's not out of line for our spouses to ask us to stop meeting with an ex-girlfriend or ex-boyfriend, or anyone for that matter. If it is causing them to feel insecure, then it is appropriate to honor their wishes for the sake of the relationship.

Security is one of the beautiful things about marriage in sickness and in health. Do what you can to remove the things that make your spouse feel insecure. Put the spotlight on your partner's needs for security—and keep it there. Stay dedicated to the one you love.

Ask your partner, "What do I do that causes you to feel secure (or insecure) in our relationship?"

She Believes in Me

As a boy growing up in Texas, I participated in an interesting phenomenon on the school playground. One boy walked to the top of a dirt mound and yelled, "King of the hill." All of us boys immediately dog-piled him. We pushed, clawed, and every now and then, even punched to claim the spot as king of the hill. Recess lasted only a few minutes, so our glory was short-lived; but to go back to class as king of the hill did something inside you. Most of the girls just watched all this happen and shook their heads. Even in elementary school they sensed this was dumb and could not understand. Yet guys love to play King of the Hill. Long after we have left the playground, we play the game in the corporate world, in relationships, and in hobbies. There is something hardwired into a man's soul that desires to conquer.

A couple of decades ago, a popular belief held that there wasn't much inherent difference between boys and girls. Toy manufacturers took these beliefs to the marketplace. They made pink and purple Lego blocks and boy dolls. Parents bought fire trucks for girls and dollhouses for boys. Guess what happened? Boys took the heads off their dolls and went to war. Girls made their fire trucks into the family van and took everyone out for a picnic. The idea had a rapid and relatively painless death.

During our wedding ceremonies, we vow to take each other in prosperity and in need. Whereas women generally need security, men need to conquer and provide. Solomon's ability to provide for the Shulammite is pictured in the opulence of the processional. She says, "King Solomon made for himself the carriage; he made it of wood from Lebanon. Its posts he made of silver, its base of gold. Its seat was upholstered with purple, its interior lovingly inlaid by the daughters of Jerusalem" (3:9, 10).

THERE IS SOMETHING HARDWIRED INTO A MAN'S SOUL THAT DESIRES TO CONQUER.

No one would question Solomon's ability to provide. The portable bed on which he rode was made from the trees of Lebanon, which would have been the best available wood in the world. Many of the furnishings of the temple and the royal palace of Solomon were built with wood from Lebanon, which is also a metaphor for beauty and fertility in the Old Testament. The picture of the groom on this portable bed becomes even richer when we look at its post, base, and seat. They were crafted from the world's most precious materials. The purple cloth was rare and represented royalty. Solomon rode in as the conquering provider to rescue his bride.

The importance of a man's need to provide is illustrated by a story the late E. V. Hill told at his wife's funeral, after she had passed away of cancer. For years Hill served as the senior pastor of Mt. Zion Missionary Baptist Church. As a young husband, E. V. was just beginning in ministry, and money was tight. One night he came home and the house was dark. His wife, Jane, had a meal all made and candles lit for a special candlelight dinner. E. V. went to the bathroom to wash up. He hit the light, but it didn't come on. Then he tried another light—nothing. He went back to the dining room and asked Jane why the lights were out, and she started to cry. "You work so hard, and we're trying, but it's pretty rough," she said. "I didn't have enough money to pay the light bill. I didn't want you to know about it, so I thought we would just eat by candlelight."

With powerful emotion E. V. commented, "She could have said, 'I've never been in this situation before. I was reared in the home of Dr. Caruthers, and we never had our lights cut off.' She could have broken my spirit; she could have ruined me; she could have demoralized me. But instead she said, 'Somehow or other we'll get these lights back on. But tonight let's eat by candlelight.'"[13] That's a woman who understood how sensitive this area of providing is for men.

A woman can hold a powerful place in a man's life. Her encouragement about his provision for the family can make or break him. Kenny Rogers recorded "She Believes in Me" from his own experience as a struggling musician trying to carve out a living. Because of a woman's faith in him, he continues on, struggling and playing, hoping that one day, one night, someone will hear a song and his career will take off.

MEN ADMIT, "I NEED TO HEAR FROM THE LADY IN MY LIFE THAT SHE BELIEVES IN ME AND WHAT I'M DOING."

Some women are frustrated by how much their husbands focus on work. Out of frustration they attack their husband's work because they want him home with the family. But when his work is attacked, he interprets that, either consciously or subconsciously, as disrespect for who he is and what he is trying to do for the family. Rather than attack him, thank him for his work for the family. Thank him for all that he does. Then lovingly encourage him to spend more time at home.

Men admit, "I need to hear from the lady in my life that she believes in me and what I'm doing." Women can show great respect to men by supporting and encouraging them in their efforts to work and provide. Just after church on Sundays, my wife tracks me down and immediately begins to meet one of my deepest needs. As a pastor, I find it challenging to connect God's Word with people on a regular basis. Over the years, Lori has become the one person whose words of comfort and kindness keep me going when I feel like giving up. I may hear encouragement from a hundred people, but I *need* to hear from one above all—my wife.

The desire to conquer reveals itself in a man's need to provide through valuable work. A woman needs to be especially careful in her comments to her husband about his income or career. These subjects can be something deeply personal for him. He may no longer be playing King of the Hill on the playground, but he needs the woman in his life to tell him that next to God, he is king of her heart.

Thank your spouse for the work he or she does to provide for the family.

Stand by Your Man (or Woman)

What is the number one country song of all time? Country Music Television recently enlightened us with their top pick—"Stand by Your Man." This classic recorded by Tammy Wynette declares a woman's commitment to her man. It was released to great praise in 1968, even though some feminist groups complained. Hillary Clinton raised some eyebrows when she appeared on *60 Minutes* after the alleged Bill Clinton affair in 1992 and said, "I'm not sitting here as some little woman standing by my man like Tammy Wynette." Tammy didn't take too kindly to that and fired back that Mrs. Clinton had "offended every true country music fan and every person who has made it on their own with no one to take them to a White House."[14] Later they made up, and when Tammy passed away, the Clintons issued a statement saying she was a legend.

Why is this song the greatest country song ever? It points to the deep needs for commitment and faithfulness that both men and women possess. This is why we take vows to last "till death do us part."

In the Song of Solomon, the Shulammite describes the day she and her partner committed themselves to one another: "Come out, you daughters of Zion, and look at King Solomon wearing the crown, the crown with which his mother crowned him on the day of his wedding, the day his heart rejoiced" (3:11). In the ancient world it was not uncommon for wedding garlands to be worn as couples progressed to the ceremony. This verse says the groom's mother crowned him. Mothers held the key position in matters of the heart—so her blessing here was significant. Solomon's family celebrated and he rejoiced!

WHY IS THIS SONG THE GREATEST COUNTRY SONG EVER? IT POINTS TO THE DEEP NEEDS FOR COMMITMENT AND FAITHFULNESS THAT BOTH MEN AND WOMEN POSSESS.

Yet many who rejoiced on their wedding day no longer rejoice in their marriages. Even though people say "till death do us part," more than half of all marriages end in divorce. Some may feel like the unity candle they lit in their marriage ceremony was actually a time bomb waiting to go off.

Marriage is complicated, and I don't pretend to know what you've been through in your relationship. God's ideal is a marriage that lasts a lifetime. In the book of Malachi, God says, "I hate divorce" (2:16). God does not hate divorced *people*. He hates *divorce*. God hates what divorce does in people's lives. It tears families apart. It shreds homes to pieces. It separates parents from children. Most who have experienced the pain of divorce would agree with God. They hate the pain divorce causes. They hate the devastation divorce brings to families.

God wants marriage to be a picture of our relationship with him. That's why the Bible presents God as the groom and the church as the bride of Christ. In the book of Revelation we read of the final day when we will be in God's direct presence again: "Let us rejoice and be glad and give him glory! For the wedding of the Lamb has come, and his bride has made herself ready" (19:7).

In the frailty of our own earthly unions, we don't always keep our vows. But no matter how well or how poorly we've done in our relationships, there is one that ultimately does not fail. There is one partner who's always faithful. There is one who always stands by us—God.

If your marriage is barely hanging on, God can help you more than a book can, more than marriage principles, more than anything else the world has to offer. When you and your spouse grow God-ward, you grow closer together spiritually and emotionally.

But what if your spouse isn't ready to grow toward God? Don't let that stop you. God will honor every move you make toward him and use you as an example of his loving grace in the life of your spouse.

THERE IS ONE PARTNER WHO'S ALWAYS FAITHFUL.

Solomon rejoiced on his wedding day. Your celebration can continue today! Remember that God's love can bring healing even after great damage. Reflect on God's desire for a relationship with you and ask him to help you grow spiritually. Through him you can stand by your partner, even in difficult times, and have a thriving relationship after "I do."

If there's any part of your marriage vows you've broken, confess that today— and determine to start anew.

PLAYLIST NO. 3

SEX IN MARRIAGE

Love Me Tender

Living in the Vegas area, there are some things you can't get away from, like Elvis. He became Vegas's adopted son after selling out 837 consecutive shows at the Hilton, leaving dozens of impersonators in his wake. I know a Flying Elvi. He parachutes out of planes, lands at your party, and breaks into "Love Me Tender." That is just cool!

Some other things you can't escape in Vegas are sexual images and innuendo. They are everywhere, from the porn that people hand out on the boulevard to the advertisements on taxicabs in the suburbs. One friend rode with his teenage son behind a cab featuring the backsides of five girls in thongs. The son said, "Dad, the second rear from the right is my friend Tony's mom." Only in Vegas!

But Elvis's "Love Me Tender" can teach us about real relationships and sex. It speaks of the need for kindness and care in a relationship and gives a broader perspective than just the physical.

Couples walk into marriage with preconceived ideas about sex. If the real thing disappoints, they may become frustrated and disillusioned. There won't be a lot of tenderness going on. Often a man does not grasp a woman's emotional needs, and she doesn't grasp his physical needs; so communication breaks down. She builds resentment because all he wants is sex. He builds resentment because there is not enough sex. Or vice versa. The reality is a misunderstanding of each other's unique wiring. Every person is different, and perspectives can be reversed or altered a million ways, but sexual compatibility can be very challenging in relationships.

We've looked at the wedding of Solomon and his bride. In chapter 4 of the Song of Solomon, they describe coming together in physical intimacy. This is the most sexually charged section of the Bible, and it's here for a reason. We tend to compartmentalize our lives between the sacred and the secular. To God it is all life. He formed us as sexual beings—he invented sex.

Throughout the Song of Solomon, we see an emphasis on sexuality in marriage. The Shulammite says, "Strengthen me with raisins, refresh me with apples, for I am faint with love" (2:5). She is literally sick with love. Raisins and apples had erotic connotations in the ancient world. In the context of this overall passage, the meaning is clear—she is asking her husband to satisfy her sexual desire.

Solomon is tender as he approaches her—"His left arm is under my head, and his right arm embraces me" (2:6). He knows to be gentle and respectful. He "embraces" her, a term which could also be translated as "fondles." Just as the bedroom door is about to close, we read this refrain: "Daughters of Jerusalem, I charge you by the gazelles and by the does of the field: Do not arouse or awaken love until it so desires" (2:7).

The couple is saying to their friends, "You may desire this kind of love and relationship, but do not force it." There is a right and a wrong time for the relationship to become sexual. Studies show that the best sex occurs within the context of marriage. In 1999, the "National Health and Social Life Survey" was completed. It was considered the most complete picture of America's sex life in history. Published in the *Journal of the American Medical Association*, the results are surprising:

Sexually active singles have the most sexual problems and get the least pleasure out of sex.

Men with the most "liberal attitudes about sex" are 75 percent more likely to fail to satisfy their partners.

Married couples by far reported the happiest satisfaction with their sex lives.

The most sexually satisfied demographic group of them all: married couples between fifty and fifty-nine![15]

Sex is a physical, emotional, and spiritual gift for marriage that is enjoyed most fully in marriage. Historically, Christians have had varying views of sex. For a significant period, believers viewed sex as something acceptable only for procreation. It was more of a necessary evil than something to be enjoyed. The Jewish culture maintained a more balanced view. From biblical times to the present, they recognized that God created sex as a wonderful experience. As one rabbi recently put it, "When sexual intercourse is done for the sake of heaven, there is nothing so holy and pure. . . . God did not create anything that is ugly and shameful. If the sexual organs are said to be shameful, how can it be said that the Creator fashioned something blemished?"[16] Sex is God's creation—a good thing.

THE MOST SEXUALLY SATISFIED DEMOGRAPHIC GROUP OF THEM ALL: MARRIED COUPLES BETWEEN FIFTY AND FIFTY-NINE!

Shaunti Feldhahn wrote *For Women Only*, in which she revealed her findings after surveying and interviewing more than a thousand men to discover their inner lives. She was shocked to realize that three out of four men admitted they felt more confident and alive in other areas of life when their sex lives were good. One man said, "What happens in the bedroom really does affect how I feel the next day at the office."[17] Sex has a huge effect on a man's emotional well-being.

SEX IS A RESULT OF A HEALTHY RELATIONSHIP, NOT THE BASIS FOR IT.

For women, this is a very important area as well. Women sometimes complain of feeling as if they are simply used for sex, while others long for more emotional support. Personal history also can play an important role in a woman's sex life. Some studies suggest that up to 50 percent of women have been sexually abused in the past. There are a tremendous amount of emotional issues involved when there has been abuse. When we bring our perspectives and histories into the bedroom, things can get complicated in a hurry.

Sex is a result of a healthy relationship, not the basis for it. Studies suggest that relationships based on sex last an average of five years. When the sexual side of things is healthy in a marriage, sex will have importance, but be secondary to other things. If it is not going well, it will seem to dominate and lead to frustration in other areas.

The preceding discussion about sex serves as a backdrop to chapter 4 of the Song of Solomon. The couple enters the bedroom and awakens love within the confines of marriage and commitment. We don't need a Flying Elvi to land at our party and sing about the importance of tenderness and sensitivity in this area—the Bible addressed it thousands of years ago. God gave us this chapter in the Song of Solomon because he desires for us to understand the dimensions of physical intimacy and to experience it fully.

Rate your sex life on a scale of 1 to 10 and talk with your spouse about your rating.

I'm Too Sexy

Right Said Fred's "I'm Too Sexy" is a song written by two brothers who worked out at the same gym where some macho male models exercised. The song tells us these models have quite an elevated view of themselves—they are too sexy for their clothes and their cars, among other things. They are too sexy for New York, Milan, and Japan, and for sure they are too sexy for your party. However, I'm not sure how you become too sexy for your cat! The song is incredibly catchy as it pokes fun at a culture obsessed with external appearance.

External appearance is important in relationships. When it comes to physical intimacy, men are usually more visual and respond to sight, while women respond to sound. Much of chapter 4 of the Song of Solomon is devoted to Solomon's description of his bride's physical appearance. He explores her beauty from head to toe. "How beautiful you are, my darling," he says. "Oh, how beautiful! Your eyes behind your veil are doves. Your hair is like a flock of goats descending from Mount Gilead" (4:1).

The metaphors and images Solomon uses were familiar to his time and place in history. Through our twenty-first century lenses, these images may seem foreign at best and insulting at worst. But let's take another look. Gilead was one of the most beautiful places in Palestine. To see a flock of black goats come down from Mount Gilead, with their hair flowing in the wind, was an exotic, jaw-dropping experience.

Maybe she's letting her hair down, and he's using the comparison to tell her how beautiful her hair is, like a "flock of goats descending from Mt. Gilead." Now guys, you may not want to use this line verbatim. An intended compliment loses some steam when you have to backtrack and explain, but an appropriate compliment goes a long way.

Solomon goes on to describe that his wife is way too sexy to need an orthodontist: "Your teeth are like a flock of sheep just shorn, coming up from the washing. Each has its twin; not one of them is alone" (4:2). The ancient world didn't have dental offices or teeth-whitening capabilities. If someone had a perfect smile, it was a big deal. Solomon is saying, "My girl has every one of her teeth, and they are white, like a sheep that's just been washed."

THINK BACK TO YOUR DAYS OF DATING. MOST LIKELY, YOU BOTH TOOK GREAT CARE TO LOOK YOUR BEST.

Solomon says her "lips are like a scarlet ribbon" (4:3). Women did use some cosmetics in the ancient world, as they do today. Solomon loves to look at her red lips. He wants more than anything to kiss the lips that delight his eyes. The shape of her face and cheeks inspire him as well. They have a reddish hue, like that of a pomegranate. He says, "Your temples behind your veil are like the halves of a pomegranate" (4:3). Her neck is described as elegant and powerful like a strong tower (4:4). The shields and weapons decorating the tower remind him of the glimmering necklace on her neck. She is graceful and everything he desires. "Your two breasts are like two fawns," he says, "like twin fawns of a gazelle that browse among the lilies. Until the day breaks and the shadows flee, I will go to the mountain of myrrh and to the hill of incense" (4:5, 6). Everything about her is in perfect symmetry. He longs to make love to her all night, "until the day breaks and the shadows flee."

Moved and motivated by the beauty of her physical features, he undresses her verbally. Yet we can't tell what she looks like from his description. Beauty is in the eye of the beholder, and there is no question of his appreciation for her. To him, she is incredibly sexy.

Solomon's visual attraction reminds us of the importance of physical appearance. Think back to your days of dating. Most likely, you both took great care to look your best. You may have gone to the gym, watched your weight, and carefully picked out your clothes. Before a date, he showered, splashed on cologne, and combed his hair. She took time to do her makeup and get everything just right. You both wanted to make an impression and be attractive to the other.

Then came love, then came marriage, then came the husband unshaven and wearing the same old shirt despite having gained twenty pounds. The worst part—he still thinks he has it going on. He can't understand why she comes out of the bathroom wearing the "It is not going to happen tonight" sleepwear. If he wants to see the lingerie, he may have to clean up his act and show that he cares about his own appearance as much as hers.

And there is something he may not be telling her. He cares deeply about her taking care of her appearance. We're not talking about looking like a supermodel. Physical appearance is an incredibly sensitive area for men and women, as evidenced by the many eating disorders and psychological problems we see in our culture. Everyone wrestles with this one. I read that even most supermodels struggle with low self-esteem when it comes to their appearance.

The issue is not, however, about looking a particular way or weighing a particular amount. It is about making an effort. In Shaunti Feldhahn's survey of over a thousand men, five out of ten said that what mattered more than results was that their wives put forth an effort to take care of themselves.[18] A man tends to interpret a lack of effort about appearance as a lack of care, not only for her, but for him as well. I know we think it shouldn't matter what a person looks like on the outside, but it *does* matter.

Some women can easily slip into a "mom routine" with their appearance. They dress super casually, stop putting on makeup, and are consumed with just navigating the details and craziness of life. I understand there is a place for that. But women also need to realize that men are motivated visually and they want you to make an effort regularly. When Lori and I had our first child, she got into a routine of wearing jogging suits—all the time. There was a jogging suit for each day of the week. I didn't want to say anything to her because I was afraid it would hurt her feelings. Then one day we sat in a marriage seminar together and the teacher said, "Moms, don't just wear the same old jogging suits every day. Take care of your appearance." Externally I casually nodded. Internally I jumped up and down thinking, *YES! Burn the jogging pants!* This can be a very important issue for men.

FIVE OUT OF TEN SAID THAT WHAT MATTERED MORE THAN RESULTS WAS THAT THEIR WIVES PUT FORTH AN EFFORT TO TAKE CARE OF THEMSELVES.

There's a strange phenomenon I've witnessed after seeing some couples go through crisis and then divorce. A year later they are dating other people, and they look like different human beings. He's hitting the gym and looking buff after losing twenty pounds. She's got a new haircut and wardrobe and looks terrific. I can't help but wonder why they didn't take the time and effort to look that good while they were together.[19]

What can you do to take better care of your physical appearance? It's not about money. I'm not talking about cosmetic surgery. You can definitely make physical improvements without spending a lot. Think about what you can do and then take active steps to make improvements. After all, if you are going to be too sexy for your car or cat, the time is now, and the person to do it for is your spouse!

Plan an intimate night with your spouse this week.

In Your Eyes

"From office affairs to internet hookups, more wives are cheating too." So read the *Newsweek* cover story, "The New Infidelity." The article chronicled the pressures women face and how more are having affairs. One thirty-nine-year-old woman who became involved with another man said, "I can't remember the last time my husband complimented me." Of her affair she said, "There is so much passion in our relationship. He tells me my skin is soft and my hair smells good. I know it sounds stupid but that stuff matters. It makes me feel sexy again."[20]

A woman has an affair with a guy more because he is emotionally available than for any other reason. She has a tremendous need for emotional support. There is a high likelihood that, if her husband does not meet this need in her life, she will find other ways to get the need met. For some women, this means finding other *people* to meet their needs.

"HUSBANDS, IN THE SAME WAY BE CONSIDERATE AS YOU LIVE WITH YOUR WIVES."

In the Bible, God acknowledges a woman's need for emotional support. Peter writes, "Husbands, in the same way be considerate as you live with your wives" (1 Peter 3:7). The phrase "live with" means literally "to dwell together." These words imply more than living in the same house. Dwelling together carries with it the idea of emotional support through a close, personal relationship. There is an honoring and cherishing that happens when two people are dwelling together.

When you honor something, you treat it as if it had great value. In the Song, Solomon proactively honors and cherishes his wife. After describing her amazing features he says, "All beautiful you are, my darling. There is no flaw in you" (4:7). While a man is often more motivated by what he sees, a woman is often motivated by what she hears. We all need to take care with our words, but men in particular should be aware that the ladies in their lives will be greatly impacted by the words that are spoken to them. This applies to both wives and daughters. Men must consistently ensure that the women they love maintain healthy self-images.

MEN CAN'T UNDERESTIMATE THE POWER OF THEIR WORDS.

I make a habit of telling my young daughter that she's beautiful inside and out. I'm always telling her that. If you ask her who is beautiful, she'll say "I am." There is no humility in that girl, but I don't care. When she hits the teen years, she'll struggle with low self-esteem and inadequacy, so I'm going to pour love and acceptance into her life now. The same goes for my wife. I don't want her to feel accepted, loved, or valued by anyone else more than she feels accepted, loved, and valued by me.

Sometimes a woman may have a hard time with personal acceptance and self-esteem because many things in our culture tell her she is not beautiful enough. From airbrushed models on magazine covers to Hollywood actresses on the big screen, messages about how women should look bombard her daily. And maybe a comment her parents or grandparents made to her about her appearance has never been forgotten. Or perhaps verbal or physical abuse occurred in the past. It could simply be the tape that plays in her mind, over and over again, saying she is not attractive. Men can't underestimate the power of their words. Whether positive or negative, the things they say will make an impact. Just as wives can carry the sword of influence when it comes to sex, men can yield power with words and either affirm or devastate their wives.

Note that Solomon doesn't simply say his wife is beautiful. He describes her beauty in specific ways. He praises her hair, lips, cheeks, and neck. He holds nothing back in letting her know how much he cares for her. When was the last time you told the love of your life that her hair smelled good? That her skin was soft? That you love her eyes?

Peter Gabriel's "In Your Eyes" is a classic from the '80s that overflows with passion and emotion. The song was featured in the movie *Say Anything,* in which John Cusack's character plays his boom box over his head to win the love of the girl, played by Ione Skye. Though it cost the producers $200,000 for the rights to use the song, this became one of the most famous movie scenes in history. The song proclaims the meaning, heat, and light one person finds in the eyes of another. It inspires us to let our spouses know how much they bring to our lives.

As I read Solomon's words to his wife, I see passion and commitment. She has no doubt about how he feels. If he keeps telling her of her beauty, she'll never feel a need for another man to tell her that her skin is soft or that her hair smells good. She'll feel invigorated by his love!

Think about the lengths people go to to have an affair. They take great pains to hide it. They carry this secret burden, cover it up with deception, live two lives, and become tense and paranoid. They do all that for someone they're not even committed to. What would happen if you took that kind of effort and energy and poured it into your marriage relationship? What if you had an affair with your marriage partner?[21] You could have the suspense, passion, and joy without the deception, guilt, and pain. So, what are you waiting for? Tell your partner what you see in his or her eyes.

Take a lesson from Solomon— write your spouse a love letter and drop it in the mail.

Behind Closed Doors

Christian psychologist Dr. Willard Harley illustrates the need for sexual intimacy by writing of a woman standing next to a glass of water, which serves as a metaphor for sexual fulfillment. A man stands beside her and desperately wants a drink, but she is between him and the glass of water. She is the only one who can give him a drink. He says, "Hey, honey, how 'bout a drink of water tonight? I'm really thirsty."

"Not tonight," she replies, "I'm not in the mood, and I have a lot of stuff going on."

Several days later, he tries again. "Hey, honey, how about you and me and the water tonight?"

"No," she says, "I have a headache."

A couple more days go by, and he's dying of thirst. "Honey," he says, "Can I PLEASE have a drink of water? I need the water. Give me a drink!"

She turns to him and says, "You're not getting any water with that kind of attitude!"

So he comes back a few days later and says, "Pleasssssssse can I have a drink?"

"OK, fine," she huffs. "Here, take it."[22]

He gets to quench his thirst, but it's bittersweet. He knows he'll get thirsty again and wonders what will happen the next time. As the illustration shows, a person's sexual need is very important. Sexual intimacy is a huge physical and emotional need particularly for men, but in some cases the roles reverse.

HE NEEDS TO BE INTIMATE WITH HER AS MUCH AS SHE NEEDS TO COMMUNICATE VERBALLY WITH HIM.

Solomon complimented his wife's beauty. He described her from top to bottom, and then he issued an invitation to sexual intimacy. "Come with me from Lebanon, my bride, come with me from Lebanon. Descend from the crest of Amana, from the top of Senir, the summit of Hermon, from the lions' dens and the mountain haunts of the leopards" (4:8). He desires to be with his wife, but she is described as being in the distant mountains of Lebanon, away from his grasp. She is inaccessible to his embrace. The imagery suggests she is not in the mood for sex, and I can almost hear in the background, "Not tonight, dear, I have a headache!"

Women may think it's no big deal when they are not in the mood. But to men, it constitutes rejection, broadcasting loud and clear that something is wrong with them, not simply with the sex. If this continues, he interprets her disinterest as a lack of love. She believes she's telling him she loves him in all kinds of ways, and their lack of intimacy has nothing to do with it. Yet this is the primary way many men receive love. The heartbreak he experiences when his wife turns him down continually is real—deep and emotional. He may not be willing to formulate the feelings into words, but they are there.

Imagine the frustration a woman feels if her husband does not talk with her for days or weeks. Every time she mentions that she'd like to talk, he says, "I can't. I have a headache." Will she buy it if he says his love for her hasn't changed, and he's just not in the mood to talk?

Women might say, "That's not the same thing." But it is. He needs to be intimate with her as much as she needs to communicate verbally with him.

Jill Eggleton Brett wrote an article entitled "Not Tonight, Dear . . ." In it she tells of how she realized the importance of this need in her husband's life.

> I felt what I did all day was meet other people's needs. Whether it was caring for my children, working in ministry, or washing my husband's clothes, by the end of the day I wanted to be done need-meeting. I wanted my pillow and a magazine. But God prompted me: *Are the "needs" you meet for your husband the needs he wants met?*
>
> If our daughters weren't perfectly primped, he didn't complain. If the kitchen floor needed mopping, he didn't say a word. And if he didn't have any socks to wear, he simply threw them in the washer himself.
>
> I soon realized I regularly said "no" to the one thing he asked of me. . . . I'd been so focused on what I wanted to get done and what my children needed, I'd cut my hubby out of the picture."[23]

BEHIND CLOSED DOORS IS A SACRED AND SPECIAL TIME TO BRING REFRESHMENT TO ONE ANOTHER.

Women wield a great deal of power over men in this area. Some use their sexuality to manipulate and get what they want, but manipulation in any form is divisive in a marriage. Seek to meet each other's needs in a healthy and loving way for joint gain, not personal gain. Don't always wait for the other person's advances. Take the initiative and approach one another sexually. One mom wrote a letter to her daughter for her wedding day. Among other things, the letter advised the young bride to "always be a lady except in the bedroom; there and only there, you can be a temptress."

Behind closed doors is your time together as a couple. The Bible challenges you to "not deprive each other" sexually (1 Corinthians 7:5). You are the only one who can truly satisfy your spouse's sexual needs. Behind closed doors is a sacred and special time to bring refreshment to one another. Use the time to reach out in a way that honors God.

Tell your spouse the top two things you enjoy most when being physically intimate.

Wonderful Tonight

Eric Clapton wrote "Wonderful Tonight" while waiting for his girlfriend and future wife to get ready for a night out. She kept changing clothes, and rather than be frustrated, Clapton channeled his energy into drafting the song. If that wasn't romantic enough, the day after their wedding he called her onstage in Tucson and sang it to her.

Romance is something very important to relationships. Women may be surprised to learn that men also desire romance. The problem is that many feel inadequate in this area. While some men aren't romantic because of busyness or laziness, others refuse to take what constitutes a huge relational risk for them.

Solomon invited his wife to be sexually intimate with him, but she was not ready. Rather than give up, he turned on the romance by openly discussing his feelings with her. "You have stolen my heart, my sister, my bride; you have stolen my heart with one glance of your eyes, with one jewel of your necklace. How delightful is your love, my sister, my bride! How much more pleasing is your love than wine, and the fragrance of your perfume than any spice" (4:9, 10). The word "sister" here is a term of affection; she is not his actual sister. He opens up about what is going on in his inner world, declaring that she has stolen his heart, and her love is better than wine, her fragrance better than any spice.

Women say one of their greatest frustrations is that their men don't open up about their feelings. A woman desperately wants to know what is going on in her partner's mind. She wants to know his thoughts and struggles. When a man takes a risk and opens up about his feelings, he serves her in a significant way, and causes her to feel loved. Someone said, "Women need to feel loved before they can make love, and men need to make love before they can feel loved." By sharing his feelings, Solomon not only causes her to feel loved, he also allows her to emotionally prepare for intimacy.

Men sometimes flake out on expressing their feelings. A guy may say, "I wasn't raised in a family where we expressed our feelings." He blames his parents and thinks he doesn't have to learn how to express himself. Yet expressing feelings is a learned action, just like mastering a golf swing. It takes practice, patience, and effort, but the man's reward is that he becomes more attractive to his mate.

Ask what your partner considers to be romantic. Each person will have a different perspective. Lori appreciates roses, but not just any roses from the grocery store. When I buy her roses from an actual florist, that communicates volumes. The key thing in romance is not that the man is smooth and perfect, but that he puts forth an effort. She'll be moved just by the fact that he is trying. A little romance sprinkled through the day increases the odds of other things happening a hundredfold. When romance increases, there is a high likelihood that sex will increase. Make an effort to meet her romantic needs. And women, reward your men for their efforts!

Relational faithfulness also enhances the sense of romance and intimacy. Solomon communicates to his wife that she is the only one for him and comments on her faithfulness to him. He says, "You are a garden locked up, my sister, my bride; you are a spring enclosed, a sealed fountain" (4:12). She is "locked" and "sealed," inaccessible to all except her husband. These terms speak to her virginity. She gives herself only to him.

Later in life Solomon would have many wives and concubines and would disobey God's commands. I believe that is why he comes full circle as an old man and returns to the same imagery of a fountain, challenging people to remain with the wife of their youth. He writes, "Drink water from your own cistern, running water from your own well. Should your springs overflow in the streets, your streams of water in the public squares? Let them be yours alone, never to be shared with strangers. May your fountain be blessed, and may you rejoice in the wife of your youth" (Proverbs 5:15-18). A husband's sexual affections are "streams" and "springs." They are not to overflow in the streets, meaning he is to be faithful to his wife sexually. The husband and wife are to please one another, like a serene well and a smooth stream. Solomon learned the hard way the importance of faithfulness to one wife, and he returns to the theme here.

"WOMEN NEED TO FEEL LOVED BEFORE THEY CAN MAKE LOVE, AND MEN NEED TO MAKE LOVE BEFORE THEY CAN FEEL LOVED."

When it comes to drinking water "from your own cistern," it should be said that there are other ways that a person can be unfaithful. For instance, one area that destroys intimacy is pornography. Pornography is a problem for both men and women, whether it is visual pornography such as adult movies or magazines, or nonvisual pornography such as certain romance novels and erotic literature. The temptation of pornography is to have one's needs met outside of the marriage.

While both men and women can be tempted by pornography, the majority of people who struggle in this area are men. I've yet to meet a woman who does not feel cheated at some level when her husband uses pornography. She can't help but interpret his actions as a lack of satisfaction with her. Some husbands pressure their wives to watch pornography and perform in similar ways. But this is often devastating to the sense of faithfulness and trust a woman needs. In the end, there is a high likelihood she will feel used as time goes on.

A LITTLE ROMANCE SPRINKLED THROUGH THE DAY INCREASES THE ODDS OF OTHER THINGS HAPPENING A HUNDREDFOLD.

Instead of looking outside the marriage relationship, place your spouse first in your heart and seek to meet each other's needs. Then you will find romance and intimacy growing to mature levels. So turn on the romance. Open up about your feelings. Guys, even if you don't have any feelings, use the phrase *I feel* regularly! Too often we start out a relationship by opening up with our feelings, but then we forget that the way we fell in love will be the way to stay in love. Many couples begin with lots of romance, and many older couples have rediscovered one another, but the in-between years can be a challenge. Realize how important romance is for your relationship, and take some steps to make it happen now. Tell your spouse that he or she looks "wonderful tonight."

Pick up a copy of *Simply Romantic Nights* by Dennis Rainey. It will give you many creative ideas for romance.

Celebration

When was the last time you heard Kool & the Gang's "Celebration"? Was it at the ballpark when someone hit a home run? at a wedding reception? on the soundtrack of *Toy Story 2*? Twenty years after it topped the charts, Kool & the Gang's tune is still everywhere—an anthem for any time people are celebrating. And it's an anthem that applies within the Song of Solomon as well.

We have seen Solomon desire to be intimate with his wife. However, she was reluctant. So he continued to romance her. The Shulammite then responds by saying, "Awake, north wind, and come, south wind! Blow on my garden, that its fragrance may spread abroad. Let my lover come into his garden and taste its choice fruits" (4:16). I don't think this passage needs a lot of commentary! She is ready and willingly invites her mate to approach her. Her fruits and spices are now available to Solomon, and the result is mutual intimacy.

In the original language, 4:16 is the exact center of the Song of Solomon. From a poetic standpoint, the middle of the Song of Solomon is the mutual celebration of sex behind the closed doors of the bedroom. The highest point of the Song, this spiritual piece of literature, is the ecstasy of intimacy. Our sexuality is wired into our souls, which is why it is much more than just a physical act; it's also a spiritual act.

After they have experienced physical intimacy, Solomon comments, "I have come into my garden, my sister, my bride; I have gathered my myrrh with my spice. I have eaten my honeycomb and my honey; I have drunk my wine and my milk" (5:1). They belong to one another. He describes their lovemaking as enjoying all of the good things of his bride.

When Solomon and his bride respond mutually, there is joy. In 5:1 we read, "Eat, O friends, and drink; drink your fill, O lovers." Who is speaking here? It doesn't seem likely that it would be the refrain of the friends, because they weren't in the bedroom with them. No one was in the bedroom with them except God himself. Many commentators propose that this is God's voice, his stamp of approval. It follows immediately after their intimate moment and the pinnacle of the Song of Solomon. It would be just like God to affirm something he created. Sexual intimacy is his gift to every marriage. He wants you and your spouse to celebrate it within the proper framework.

THE HIGHEST POINT OF THE SONG, THIS SPIRITUAL PIECE OF LITERATURE, IS THE ECSTASY OF INTIMACY.

In *Sacred Marriage*, Gary Thomas notes an unusual place where prayer and sex are mentioned together in the Bible. Paul says, "Do not deprive each other except by mutual consent and for a time, so that you may devote yourselves to prayer" (1 Corinthians 7:5).

This is usually interpreted to say that sex distracts us from prayer. Yet it is really important where the comma is placed here. Gordon Fee, one of the brightest Bible scholars in America, suggests Paul is saying *abstinence* in a marriage can hinder our prayers. When a man or a woman is too distracted by sexual urges left unfulfilled due to abstinence, then his or her focus is taken off prayer. Paul is saying, "Have physical relations so that your needs are met, and your mind and heart will be free to focus on prayer and knowing God." Now, this doesn't mean a man should say, "Honey, will you please help my prayer life tonight?" But it is an interesting spin on prayer. The sexual side of things and the spiritual side of things can work together. Married couples can completely give themselves to one another so they can completely give themselves to God.[24]

In the bedroom, people have many questions about what is OK and what is not OK. Solomon and his wife engage all the senses in physical intimacy: sight, smell, taste, touch, and sound. Due to the nature of poetry, there are not lots of details. When I have done marriage counseling, I've been asked lots of questions about where the boundaries are for a Christian couple. Some wonder about oral sex and other practices. The tough thing about this is that the Bible does not provide us with specific guidelines as far as what is appropriate for married sexual relations. So let me share some questions pastor and author Jimmy Evans developed in his book *Marriage on the Rock* to help determine whether something is appropriate:

> 1. Does this increase oneness and intimacy?
> 2. Is it mutually pleasurable or at least mutually agreed upon? (Spouses should not be forced to do anything against their wills.)
> 3. Is it hygienically and physically safe?
> 4. Can I do this with a clear conscience before God? (God is not a prude, and he is not embarrassed by sex. However, according to Scripture, if we cannot do something by faith, it is sin.)
> 5. Is this something I would want my children to practice in their marriages someday?[25]

MARRIED COUPLES CAN COMPLETELY GIVE THEMSELVES TO ONE ANOTHER SO THEY CAN COMPLETELY GIVE THEMSELVES TO GOD.

These questions can bring clarity to different sexual practices in a relationship. So "Eat, O friends, and drink; drink your fill, O lovers." You don't need Kool & the Gang to celebrate God's wonderful gift.

Take a moment to thank God for the gift of sex.

FIGHTING FAIR

PLAYLIST NO. 4

Emotional Rollercoaster

Over the years, people have opted for some interesting ways to tie the knot. In Tampa, Florida, fifteen couples married on a roller coaster. The guys wore tuxedos, and the girls wore wedding dresses. Each of them was fitted with a microphone and a headset so they could hear the vows and legally respond. What these couples didn't know is that once the roller coaster stopped, the relationship ride was just beginning.

A roller-coaster ride is an apt description for a marriage, with its highs and lows. There are times of great peace and joy, and times of unsettling conflict and tension. The fact that we are humans makes conflict inevitable. So if we can't avoid it, the next best thing to do is to grow in our relationships and learn to navigate those times of friction and discord.

One night I came home from work feeling stressed out and tired. I wasn't in a good frame of mind, and I needed sleep. When I walked in, our kids were amped up like they'd been on an IV of sugar all day. It felt like the inmates were taking over the asylum, and so I was rather short with the kids. Needless to say, this didn't sit well with my wife, who shot me "the look" and corrected me. Love was not in the air!

What did I do? I did what any brainless guy does: I left the room. Now, just for the record, it's rarely wise to leave the room during conflict. I went to the bedroom, shut the door, and spent some time reading, unwinding, and cooling off. Lori, on the other hand, was downstairs with no escape valve. She couldn't believe that after this incident, I left the room. What kind of insensitive action is that? Not only did I leave the room, I left her with the kids, whom she had already managed all day.

That night a cloud of tension hung over the Wilhite house. We put the kids to bed and said no more than six words to each other. When we got into bed, she went for her corner, and I went for mine. It felt like the whole state of Texas was between us.

"I SLEPT BUT MY HEART WAS AWAKE."

On my side of the state I thought, *Maybe we can just go to sleep and forget about it. Tomorrow morning everything will be fine.* I rationalized that I shouldn't start a conversation, because it could be an hour long, putting it well beyond midnight before I got to sleep.

On her side, the storm raged. She clenched her pillow and thought, *He'd better not go to sleep without apologizing. He's in big trouble if he doesn't talk about it.* In the midst of the storm, neither of us was willing to take shelter in the arms of the other.

So far, we've seen some pretty good highs in the relationship of Mr. and Mrs. Solomon. When we left them last, they were having a great night in the bedroom, complete with God's divine stamp of approval. But alas, they are only human. As we move into chapter 5 of the Song of Solomon, the couple goes from a great night in the bedroom to a really bad one. Chapters 5 and 6 reveal a conflict that erupts in their relationship as they hit a low point.

In the Song she says, "I slept but my heart was awake" (5:2). Maybe they got into an argument and he walked out. Perhaps she shot him "the look" and he didn't deal with that very well. Maybe he told her he'd be home for dinner, but he showed up several hours late. Whatever had happened, she was tossing and turning in bed, replaying the scene over and over in her mind.

Ever have trouble sleeping when there is tension in your relationship? You're in bed, half asleep, but you are upset. You're angry. You can't believe your spouse did this or said that. You try to sleep, but your dreams don't bring peace. That is exactly where the Shulammite was.

God inspired the inclusion of passion and intimacy in the Song. Now he includes its counterpart, the ugly but inevitable state of discord. Why? Because we're fallible. So let's take some time here to bust some myths.

Myth #1: *A good relationship is one without conflict.* Every relationship has conflict. It is normal in healthy relationships.

Myth #2: *We must resolve all serious conflicts for our relationships to thrive.* Research shows that many marriages thrive even when significant areas of conflict are never resolved. The couple simply learn how to work around their differences.

There is no one right way to face differences. Some couples are happily married for forty years, yet avoid conflict at all costs. Others are volatile and quick to raise their voices. Some remain calm and validate one another's feelings. Research does not indicate one style of conflict management that inevitably leads to a lifetime together. Whatever style you use must work for both of you.

MYTH #1: A GOOD RELATIONSHIP IS ONE WITHOUT CONFLICT.

Dr. Gottman describes the major things couples resort to in conflict as the "Four Horsemen of the Apocalypse": defensiveness, stonewalling, criticism, and contempt. The primary one that becomes a determining factor is contempt. He says:

> You would think that criticism would be the worst, because criticism is a global condemnation of a person's character. Yet contempt is qualitatively different from criticism. With criticism I might say to my wife, "You never listen, you are really selfish and insensitive." Well, she's going to respond defensively to that. That's not very good for our problem solving and interaction. But if I speak from a superior plane, that's far more damaging, and contempt is any statement made from a higher level. A lot of the time it's an insult . . . "You're scum." It's trying to put that person on a lower plane than you. It's hierarchical.[26]

So goes contempt, so goes the relationship. This all points to how important it is that we learn to deal with conflict in a healthy way.

As for Lori and me, we eventually said we were sorry and reconciled. Neither of us could stand the tension as we clung to our sides of the bed. Conflict is inevitable, so I'm grateful God included this issue in the Song. Let's look at some principles for dealing with resolvable conflicts and for moving on despite continual debates.

Are there traces of contempt in your speech that need to be eliminated? If so, what are they?

Hit Me with Your Best Shot

"Hit Me with Your Best Shot" became a huge hit for Pat Benatar. Eddie Schwartz wrote the song, and described how it came to him this way: "I was in a kind of weird therapy when I was in my mid-twenties. . . . One of the things we did was punch pillows, I guess it had something to do with getting out hostility. I went to a session where we punched the pillows for a while. It all seemed kind of strange, but I remember walking outside of this therapy session and standing on the doorstep of the building I'd been in, this small house in Toronto, and the title just came to me, 'Hit Me with Your Best Shot.' . . . I haven't been to therapy before or since. Maybe I should go back."[27] The song was always meant to be taken metaphorically, with no actual hitting going on. But it became a cry of self-confidence in the face of all kinds of difficulties.

In relationships, there are times when the verbal blows are flying and tension fills the air. Mr. and Mrs. Solomon faced plenty of conflict. We saw in the last chapter that something had come between them. It was common in their culture for couples to sleep in different chambers. After the conflict she's gone to her chamber for the night, and she can't sleep. He comes knocking on her door seeking reconciliation, love, and affection. "Listen!" she says. "My lover is knocking." Solomon says, "Open to me, my sister, my darling, my dove, my flawless one" (5:2).

Now doesn't that just sound like a guy who's in trouble?

Only a few verses ago she had said, "Awake, north wind, and come, south wind! Blow on my garden" (4:16). Now look at her response. "I have taken off my robe," she says, "must I put it on again? I have washed my feet—must I soil them again?" (5:3). You can almost hear the exasperation in her voice. She has no intention of getting up and coming to the door. After all, she'd have to put her robe on to do it! Her feet might get a little dirty. You could cut the tension in the air with a knife.

So how do we fight fair in love's crazy conflicts?

One way is to tackle the problem, not each other. When we get into an argument, it escalates as we go after each other. We get defensive and fight back, forgetting that we are on the same team. We treat our partners more like enemies than best friends. Fixing blame instead of the problem, we allow little things to escalate into significant issues.

"OPEN TO ME, MY SISTER, MY DARLING, MY DOVE, MY FLAWLESS ONE." NOW DOESN'T THAT JUST SOUND LIKE A GUY WHO'S IN TROUBLE?

One guy was frustrated with his wife for never changing the toilet tissue roll. He would accuse, "You never change the toilet tissue roll!" She'd fire back, "I change it just as much as you do!" So he set out to prove his case against her. Every time he replaced the toilet roll, he took the cardboard cylinder, dated it, and stored it in a paper bag. He stockpiled for war. Eventually an argument erupted, and she threw some complaint in his face. He returned to his favorite pet peeve: "You never change the toilet tissue roll like I ask you to!"

"I do it just as much as you do!" she retorted.

"No you don't, and I'll prove it," he replied smugly. He walked over to the closet, pulled out his bag of cardboard cylinders, and poured them out on the floor. "See," he said with pride, "I told you I change it more than you do." (This is not a smart man.)

"You're sick!" she said with disgust.

Now that really upset him. He had a plan and had proved his case, but he needed an objective person who would side with him. So he called a psychiatrist and set an appointment. The couple got in the car, taking along his Santa sack of cardboard cylinders. (This guy actually believed he was going to win this one.)

Inside the office, he stated his case. "I need your help," he said. "I married a woman who won't change the toilet tissue roll." He then poured out all the cardboard cylinders onto the floor to prove it.

The psychiatrist looked down at the pile and said, "You're sick."

We may laugh or think this guy's extreme, but we all have small issues in our lives that we allow to become big deals. Several years ago Lori and I had an ongoing disagreement about repainting the nursery in our home. With a baby on the way, she wanted to remodel the nursery. The problem was that we'd bought an eighty-six-year-old house and completely renovated it in one and a half years. I felt burned out on renovation! Every time the conversation came up, I said, "The next thing I'm doing to this house is place a For Sale sign in the front yard!"

"But we need to remodel the nursery," Lori said.

"We just worked on the nursery, before it was the nursery," I replied.

We went back and forth until I got some great marital advice from an older couple. Over lunch I explained our dilemma. The man smiled at me and said, "Jud, sometimes you have to make a choice. You can be right, or you can be happy, but you can't be both!" Wow! We bought the paint and redid the nursery. I chose to be happy!

YOU CAN BE RIGHT, OR YOU CAN BE HAPPY, BUT YOU CAN'T BE BOTH!

Give and take is what relationships are all about. Dr. Gottman's research indicates that 69 percent of all marital conflicts are perpetual—meaning they will never be "solved."[28] Yet thousands of couples learn to thrive in spite of their differences, which is why understanding the principle of give and take is so important.

In his book *After the Honeymoon*, psychologist Dan Wile writes:

> When choosing a long-term partner . . . you will inevitably be choosing a particular set of unsolvable problems that you'll be grappling with for the next ten, twenty, or fifty years. . . .
>
> Paul married Alice and Alice gets loud at parties and Paul, who is shy, hates that. But if Paul had married Susan, he and Susan would have gotten into a fight before they even got to the party. That's because Paul is always late and Susan hates to be kept waiting. She would feel taken for granted, which she is very sensitive about. Paul would see her complaining about this as her attempt to dominate him, which he is very sensitive about. If Paul had married Gail, they wouldn't have even gone to the party because they would still be upset about an argument they had the day before about Paul's not helping with the housework. To Gail, when Paul does not help, she feels abandoned, which she is sensitive about, and to Paul, Gail's complaining is an attempt at domination, which he is sensitive about."[29]

No matter whom you are married to, there will be issues. When you are tempted to hit your spouse with your best shot, first determine how important the issue is. You may be wise to choose to be happy, rather than fight to be right! The next time you're in an argument that's escalating, remember the phrase *same team*. That one phrase helps defuse things a bit as you remember your partner is not your enemy. Change your focus to tackle the problem, not each other.

Jot down one area of tension about which you can choose to be happy, rather than fight to be right.

Love Is a Battlefield

We last left our lovers in a bad way. Solomon was knocking at the chamber door of his lovely wife, looking for a little comfort and affection. She was lying in bed and refusing his pleas to get up and open the door. Then she had a change of heart. "I arose to open for my lover, and my hands dripped with myrrh, and my fingers with flowing myrrh, on the handles of the lock," she says. "I opened for my lover, but my lover had left; he was gone. My heart sank at his departure. I looked for him but did not find him. I called him but he did not answer" (5:5, 6).

Have you ever had a marital argument escalate to the point that one of you just left the scene? Love is a battlefield. When someone goes AWOL, anger and tension suddenly give way to fear and angst. We are afraid of where she may go or what he might do in such a state of emotional distress.

After Solomon left, the Shulammite says, "My heart sank at his departure." In the original language, this same phrase is used in Genesis 38, describing people's hearts when Rachel died. In other words, this is a crisis; it is real heartbreak. He's gone, and she doesn't know where.

One thing you can do to keep arguments from getting to this point is to set some ground rules. Get together for a calm and rational conversation at a time when emotions are at an even keel, and set some guidelines for future arguments. This can keep a dispute from escalating to a major blowup like the one we see between Solomon and his bride. Here are some simple principles to consider for your ground rules.

Start the conversation gently. Paul writes, "Do not let any unwholesome talk come out of your mouths, but only what is helpful for building others up according to their needs, that it may benefit those who listen" (Ephesians 4:29).

Periodically we get a horrible smell in our car. Having small children, I always think first that a dirty diaper is hidden somewhere. One day when the smell had returned, I searched my entire car with no luck. I had strollers, jackets, toys, and everything else outside on the ground. Then I found a sippy cup under the seat. The cup contained old, hot, spoiled milk that had baked inside the car for weeks at temperatures over 150 degrees! I then did a very foolish thing only first-time parents do—I opened the sippy cup. The rankest stench I have ever smelled in my life overwhelmed me, causing me to feel completely nauseated. I almost fell down. Interestingly, the word Paul uses in the verse mentioned above, *unwholesome,* actually means "rotten or spoiled." When we speak harmful words that are intended to hurt, it is like we are opening a rank sippy cup under the noses of our spouses. We dish out spoiled milk and we often underestimate the devastating and counterproductive effect these words have. A person may take years to overcome some of these verbal blows. Now I do what all seasoned parents do when they find an old sippy cup— just throw it in the trash with a smile.

Dr. Gottman's research shows that when a conversation has a "harsh startup" that contains either contempt, disgust, or a demeaning attitude, it will usually end on a negative note as well. In fact, 96 percent of the time the first three minutes of a conflict will determine the outcome of a fifteen-minute conversation.[30] When we start by degrading one another, the conversation will usually not be beneficial and will end as it began.

When conflict occurs, keep your tone of voice level. Studies tell us that 90 percent of communication is *how* you say something, not *what* you say. The tone in which you say something has everything to do with how it's received.

Avoid comparisons. When we get into arguments we push little comparison buttons that take things to a new level. Just one volley of "You are just like your mother" and *BOOM,* it's war!

Don't leverage divorce, finances, or sex in the midst of an argument. Throwing out threats such as "If you don't do this, I'll get a divorce" only creates more problems. By doing so, you are not dealing with the problem. The only thing you *might* be achieving is winning the current battle. Is it worth it? You may win that battle, but if you continue to fight that way, your long-term odds could mean losing the war. Leveraging the ammunition of divorce, finances, or sex in the heat of an argument is damaging. And at some point, you may experience severe backfire.

"DO NOT LET ANY UNWHOLESOME TALK COME OUT OF YOUR MOUTHS, BUT ONLY WHAT IS HELPFUL FOR BUILDING OTHERS UP ACCORDING TO THEIR NEEDS, THAT IT MAY BENEFIT THOSE WHO LISTEN."

Don't run to your parents or in-laws. In some relationships it is common after an argument for the wife to call Mom and give a blow-by-blow from her perspective. When she does that regularly, what happens to Mom's opinion of the husband? All Mom hears about are his problems. Maybe the woman thinks it doesn't matter because Mom lives a thousand miles away. But what about when Mom and Dad fly in for the holidays and everyone gathers at the table as one big happy family? Is there any wonder there's tension? The end result is unnecessary drama in the family. Keep the parents and in-laws out of the pitfalls of the relationship. Then, when you come together for family gatherings, you can enjoy being a family without all the underlying bitterness and conflict.

But what about the times you just need to vent your frustrations? Find a trusted friend to help keep you grounded at those moments. Or try journaling or writing a letter (not to be mailed) to express your emotions.

Be careful with reflective listening. When counseling couples in conflict, I have often advocated reflective listening. I encourage a spouse in conflict to repeat back what he or she heard the other say. Repeating it back gives the spouse an opportunity to clarify, and it gives a chance to better understand. This is common advice among marriage therapists. Yet Neil Jacobson of the University of Washington did a study and found that techniques such as reflective listening only work 35 percent of the time.[31] In many cases, reflective listening does more harm than good. When couples are in the heat of an argument, they say hateful things. Having someone repeat back something hateful only drives the stake in further. And with all the emotions flying around, they rarely hear the intent anyway. After all, in significant conflict a person's heart rate escalates to over a hundred beats per minute! With that much adrenaline pumping through someone's veins, he or she isn't in a casual state of mind.

96 PERCENT OF THE TIME THE FIRST THREE MINUTES OF A CONFLICT WILL DETERMINE THE OUTCOME OF A FIFTEEN-MINUTE CONVERSATION.

The research does show that reflective listening is important in marriages when discussing issues *other* than the relationship. Using reflective listening to discover how your spouse is doing at work or managing the conflict of another relationship can be helpful. It just rarely works in marital conflict.

Sit down with your spouse for a calm and reasonable discussion about these ground rules for love and war. Add a few of your own. Just keep it simple, and then remember to play by the rules when a dispute arises. Perhaps by following some simple rules we can keep an argument from escalating like Solomon's.

Choose one ground rule and work to apply it in conversation.

You Wreck Me

I used to board airplanes and be annoyed if I saw small children sitting near me. When a young mom boarded with children I thought, *Oh no, please don't sit close to me.* If she did, I moved. I didn't want to be near a crying baby.

Then we had a child. The first time we boarded a plane with our baby, Lori and I walked down the aisle thinking, *I'm sorry, I'm so sorry.* Now when I see a mom climb on board with children, I view her differently. I pray for her. If her children give her fits, I smile and let her know it's OK. Why? Because once you board a plane with a child, you see everything differently.

When Tom Petty wrote "You Wreck Me," the chorus originally said "you rock me." The band thought this was too ordinary, so they changed one word, and the entire dynamic of the song was transformed. Sometimes the smallest tweaks make the largest difference in both music and marriage. Such is the case with sympathy.

Peter writes, "Finally, all of you, live in harmony with one another; be sympathetic" (1 Peter 3:8). The word translated "sympathy" has the idea of "feeling with." Once we have traveled the same road—or flown in the same plane—as others, we are able to have more compassion. When we show sympathy to another, we validate that person's feelings. We acknowledge what the person is going through.

SOMETIMES THE SMALLEST TWEAKS MAKE THE LARGEST DIFFERENCE IN BOTH MUSIC AND MARRIAGE.

Showing sympathy will go a long way to keep conflicts moving forward productively, or to avoid them altogether. For example, let's say your spouse comes to you at the end of the day and says, "I'm tired." How do you respond?

A) Recite a list of your day's activities, giving all the better reasons *you* have to be tired.

B) Give reasons why you can't imagine how your spouse could be tired. After all, she never left the house all day and probably had time for a nap; or he is in a quiet office all day and takes long lunches at expensive restaurants (which, by the way, you never get to go to).

C) Ignore his or her comment entirely and ask what's for dinner, or when the toilet will be fixed.

D) Validate your spouse's feelings.

Notice the shortest answer? I guarantee that using answer D will be followed by the calmest conversation. Arguments start over the simplest things when there is not this validation. When a spouse states his or her feelings about something, chances are the only thing wanted and needed at that particular moment is sympathy. All you have to do is validate your spouse's feelings and leave it at that. But if you launch immediately into airing your own opinions, there could be trouble. A man might say, "Oh, you think *you* got problems? Listen to this!" Then his wife becomes frustrated, not because of what he said, but because she feels ignored. Now he gets frustrated because he can tell *she's* frustrated, and things get crazier from there.

WHEN A SPOUSE STATES HIS OR HER FEELINGS ABOUT SOMETHING, CHANCES ARE THE ONLY THING WANTED AND NEEDED AT THAT PARTICULAR MOMENT IS SYMPATHY.

When conflicts begin to get crazy, men can show sympathy by saying the words "I am sorry." This is often hard for men. Guys see these words differently than women do. A man will struggle with saying these words because, to him, they imply an admission of guilt. *I'm not telling her I'm sorry*, he thinks. *I didn't do anything wrong.* But for women, saying "I am sorry" means something entirely different. To them, it's a statement of sympathy, a validation of their feelings. When a man says those words, he is showing he cares. As my wife and I lay in bed that night on opposite sides, the phrase "I am sorry" opened the door to resolution. We talked. We each expressed our feelings. And we came away with a better understanding of each other. When you do this, it moves the focus from placing blame to addressing the situation.

Women can also help show sympathy by avoiding extreme statements. A woman may use exaggeration to get to the deeper meaning of what she feels, but a man hears literally. Guys tend to exaggerate about facts and data, like how big the fish was or how fast they drove from one city to another. Women tend to exaggerate about their feelings. They can help men and foster understanding by speaking in the most concrete, black-and-white language possible. If you're feeling disconnected and want to spend some time alone together, tell him exactly that. Who knows? Maybe he'll come up with the idea of going out, once he grasps what you are saying.

So make some small adjustments in showing sympathy to one another, and perhaps your relationship will go from "you wreck me" to "you rock me!"

Repeat these
words out loud:
"I am sorry."

Cuts Like a Knife

One day my young daughter randomly started wailing. It turned out she had just noticed a little scrape on her knee that had happened hours earlier. This previously undetected scrape now became a major issue in her life. "I need a Band-Aid!" she cried. Somehow the comforting presence of a bandage brings instant healing for kids. After I applied it, the world was right again.

Wouldn't it be great if a quick-fix bandage could heal a broken heart or mend hurt feelings? If only life were that simple. The problem is, too many of us pretend it *is* that simple. We use emotional bandages as coping mechanisms to deal with our hurts and pains. We ignore problems, bury the pain, and pretend that nothing happened. *It doesn't bother me,* we tell ourselves. We slap a small bandage on problems that need real attention.

Children cry when hurt. Everyone within earshot becomes aware of the child's pain and suffering, however slight it may be. But adults use a different strategy. We buck up, internalize the hurt, and use whichever bandage fits the moment. This seems to be a phenomenon of our culture. Our society views the practice of emotional restraint as dignified.

In biblical times, this wasn't the case. People in mourning, for example, would tear their clothes and dramatically weep and cry. This wasn't for show. It was just an honest release of their emotional pain and heartbreak—perfectly acceptable in their culture. They got it all out during their days of mourning. They let their emotions hang out like the day's laundry in the fresh, clean air. It was a liberating, purifying, and healthy letting go, allowing them to then get on with life.

WOULDN'T IT BE GREAT IF A QUICK-FIX BANDAGE COULD HEAL A BROKEN HEART OR MEND HURT FEELINGS?

So am I advocating a big, dramatic scene in your household every time you get your feelings hurt? Of course not. But neither should you bury your feelings and pretend nothing has happened when you are truly hurting. Buried hurts have a propensity for surfacing in all kinds of places. They show up as uninvited guests in arguments, physical ailments, anger, depression, or even substance abuse.

What do we do when real injury occurs? The Shulammite's heart is crushed now that Solomon has gone and nobody knows where he is. She proactively searches for him. She says, "I looked for him but did not find him. I called him but he did not answer. The watchmen found me as they made their rounds in the city. They beat me, they bruised me; they took away my cloak, those watchmen of the walls!" (5:6, 7).

There are different interpretations of what it means when she says the watchmen abused her. I have a hard time thinking the watchmen abused the queen! I take this to mean the watchmen couldn't help her find her lover so she beats herself up with guilt, incredibly disappointed with herself. That they couldn't help her made her failure even more piercing. Her cloak is taken away, everything is gone, and she is left alone before God. The pain of her loneliness and loss cuts like a knife.

When we are alone before God, he does the work of spiritual heart surgery. There is no use in hiding or faking it. In that moment of honesty, healing can begin. As this woman reaches that moment, she realizes that she injured Solomon. "O daughters of Jerusalem, I charge you—if you find my lover, what will you tell him? Tell him I am faint with love" (5:8). She is saying, "Tell him that I am sorry and I love him; indicate to him that I want to reconcile."

Both Solomon and the Shulammite would need to communicate with each other about their hurts. Healing starts when you acknowledge your injury. Let's say you're at a party with your spouse. In the midst of laughing and joking with the crowd, your spouse makes a seemingly innocent but flip comment about you. Unknown to him or her, you've been badly stung. So do you talk about this at an appropriate time, or do you quickly bandage it and let it fester inside?

WHEN WE ARE ALONE BEFORE GOD, HE DOES THE WORK OF SPIRITUAL HEART SURGERY.

Emotional hurts and pains cannot be fixed by covering them up. Quick-fix bandages only aggravate wounds and prevent long-term healing. You may need to wait until you have emotionally cooled off, but when the time is right, talk with your spouse in a calm and rational way; let him or her know exactly how you feel. If you don't, the behavior is likely to happen again. Too often, a spouse will continue hurtful behavior without the knowledge or understanding of its effect on his or her partner. While the injured spouse assumes the behavior is intentional, the partner is oblivious.

Is it time to clear out your medicine cabinet? Do you need to get rid of those quick-fix bandages? Be honest with your spouse and acknowledge your injury. Lay it out there at the right time with reconciliation as your goal, and let the healing begin.

Do you have any emotional hurts you need to acknowledge to your partner? What are they?

You've Got a Friend in Me

Randy Newman's "You've Got a Friend in Me" always brings a smile to my face. The feel-good song reminds me of those on whom I can count. It also reminds me of *Toy Story* and the fun times I've had watching my kids dance around the TV to the soundtrack as the film's credits roll. And it reminds me of my daughter's favorite toys and how they are her faithful friends—always there to listen to her troubles, like when she gets her feelings hurt. The only problem is, they can't give her much helpful advice.

Wouldn't it be great to have a seasoned friend giving us direction when it comes to disputes in marriage? Before marriage, couples spend hours gazing into each other's eyes and talking about any and every subject. They share hopes and dreams, successes and failures, things that brought pain and happiness to their respective lives. So what happens after they're married and they argue? Who do they talk to? We've already discussed the inevitable fallout of sharing every fight and disagreement with Mom or Dad. But expressing our feelings to someone who cares can be a great release. Talking to an objective "coach" or third party can reveal new and helpful perspectives. The important thing is to choose wisely in selecting a friend for sideline input.

We've seen that the Shulammite found herself in a tough place. She didn't know where Solomon was, and she felt terrible about what happened. So now she seeks out wise and trusted friends—the daughters of Jerusalem. Her friends give great counsel. "How is your beloved better than others, most beautiful of women?" they ask. "How is your beloved better than others, that you charge us so?" (5:9). Their questions cause her to reflect. They don't simply agree with her side, nor do they aggravate her more by telling her how bad Solomon may have been. Instead, they help her process her thoughts and discover her true feelings.

SO WHAT HAPPENS AFTER THEY'RE MARRIED AND THEY ARGUE? WHO DO THEY TALK TO?

When we are in the midst of a conflict, it is very important that we turn to the right friends. If the woman goes to the wrong girlfriends and unloads, they're likely just to empathize and agree with her because she's a friend. "He did *what?* That's so wrong, girl!" This will only cause things to escalate even more. The same thing goes for him. If he goes to the wrong buddies, they commiserate with him: "I can't believe she did that to you! Who does she think she is?" Instead of being calmed down by friends, the couple is more upset than ever by the time they get back together. They've done nothing but gather fuel and fan the flames of the argument. Going to a seasoned person or a trusted friend who can be objective can make all the difference.

As the Shulammite reflects, she comes to this conclusion: "My lover is radiant and ruddy, outstanding among ten thousand" (5:10). She then launches into the longest list of praise and admiration in the Song of Solomon.

> His head is purest gold; his hair is wavy and black as a raven. His eyes are like doves by the water streams, washed in milk, mounted like jewels. His cheeks are like beds of

spice yielding perfume. His lips are like lilies dripping with myrrh. His arms are rods of gold set with chrysolite. His body is like polished ivory decorated with sapphires. His legs are pillars of marble set on bases of pure gold. His appearance is like Lebanon, choice as its cedars. His mouth is sweetness itself; he is altogether lovely. This is my lover, this my friend, O daughters of Jerusalem. (5:11-16)

Isn't that great? As she seeks wise counsel, she comes to the realization that she loves this guy and he is perfect for her. Tommy Nelson lists a few of the features that the Shulammite recalled about Solomon:

He was pure in his motives and behaviors toward her. Repeatedly she referred to him as white, including white as ivory and white as marble. He was extremely handsome— more handsome even than ten thousand other men combined. His head (in this case his mind) was filled with wisdom more valuable than gold. . . . He had a steadfast gaze and clear outlook toward her. His eyes were "fitly set," which means they were wide open and focused on her. He saw her, and her alone, among all other women. It is also a reference to the fact that Solomon did not have a shifty look to his eyes; his eyes did not narrow in anger or mistrust, they never openly flared in anger, and they were never bored into dullness. They were eyes of immutable kindness and unchanged blessing toward her.[32]

Solomon was strong spiritually and physically. He treated his wife with care and gentleness, but he was a guy's guy. He was the man of her dreams.

WHEN WE ARE IN THE MIDST OF A CONFLICT, IT IS VERY IMPORTANT THAT WE TURN TO THE RIGHT FRIENDS.

I have found that seeking counsel from an older couple or a more seasoned person is invaluable. Think about people you know at church or elsewhere who have been down the road of life and have wisdom. Ask them if, maybe once a month or once a quarter, you could buy them a meal and talk about how they get through the trials of their marriage. I've collected some of the best marital advice that way.

There are times in a relationship when we need more than our friends and mentors can reasonably provide. When your marriage hits a dark time, you may need to seek professional help. Don't be embarrassed to call a Christian counselor for guidance. If you think you can't afford it, ask yourself some questions. Can you afford to lose this person you love so much? Can you afford to see your family devastated by a breakup? Can you afford to walk away from all the things you've shared in life? Perhaps you can't afford *not* to pay for good counsel.

So remember Randy Newman's advice for when the road appears rough and the troubles seem to overwhelm. Call on a trusted friend who can help. No matter how tough things get, "you've got a friend in me."

> Talk with your spouse about developing a relationship with someone who can give you wise relational counsel.

Give a Little Bit

When Lori was six months pregnant, she sat down on the couch and ripped the seam down the rear of her pants. There are several ways to react when a woman blows out her pants. I began to giggle and then laugh uncontrollably. She placed her hands over her face, and I thought she was laughing too. We were one big "ha ha" family, until she made the noise—the deep gasp of someone weeping. At that point I realized her hands were not over her face because of the moment's sheer delight.

In the recesses of my mind a voice grew louder: "You messed up bad, Jud." So I immediately shifted into, "Lori, you're not fat, I mean, uh, it's the pants they just . . . uh . . . it's OK, you're pregnant."

Lori cried as I tried to bring comfort. Eventually she cried so hard, she threw up. I'm not talking about a small incident. She threw up so hard that she broke blood vessels across her face. Every time I looked at her over the next week I was reminded—*I am a LOSER husband!* I needed grace from Lori, and unfortunately for her, I've needed grace practically every day she has known me. I'm grateful she willingly forgives. Without consistent forgiveness, our relationship would collapse.

Roger Hodgson wrote "Give a Little Bit" while with the band Supertramp. The song is about giving care, compassion, and forgiveness to those we love. Hodgson said, "If you show that you care and reach out, it really makes a difference. It is very surprising the response that you receive—most often it will be love, happiness, and gratitude."[33]

FORGIVENESS MAY EVEN SEEM IMPOSSIBLE, BUT THE SOONER YOU BEGIN THE JOURNEY TOWARD FORGIVENESS, THE SOONER YOU WILL EXPERIENCE FREEDOM.

In the Song of Solomon, the Shulammite eventually finds Solomon. How does Solomon respond? Does he rub it in her face and say, "I can't believe you wouldn't open the door for me that night?" Does he pile on more guilt and pain? No, he chooses to give a bit of his love. He says, "You are beautiful, my darling. . . . Turn your eyes from me; they overwhelm me. Your hair is like a flock of goats descending from Gilead" (6:4). Does that sound familiar? He goes through the same list of loving compliments that he'd given her in the honeymoon phase of their relationship, when he said her eyes were like doves and her neck like the tower of David. He reaffirms his love, lets go of the grudge, and moves forward in the relationship.

People have a nasty habit of holding grudges. I have counseled people so caught up in their grudges, they can't see their own responsibility. They blame everything on someone or something else—parents, children, spouse, relatives, or job. They are consumed with bitterness and refuse to deal with the truth. Until they make an effort to come to a place of forgiveness toward others, they will never be happy. Never. I understand that forgiveness is extremely difficult. Coming to forgive someone is a process, especially if the hurts run deep. Forgiveness may even seem impossible, but the sooner you begin the journey toward forgiveness, the sooner you will experience freedom.

Jesus links our own forgiveness with the way we forgive others in the strongest language: "For if you forgive men when they sin against you, your heavenly Father will also forgive you. But if you do not forgive men their sins, your Father will not forgive your sins" (Matthew 6:14, 15).

We do not earn God's forgiveness by forgiving others, but the surest sign that we have been forgiven is the way we forgive others. One of Satan's strategies to hinder our relationships is to encourage and exploit a lack of forgiveness. "I have forgiven in the sight of Christ for your sake," writes Paul, "in order that Satan might not outwit us. For we are not unaware of his schemes" (2 Corinthians 2:10, 11). Satan's schemes are directly linked to keeping us from forgiveness.

AS CORRIE TEN BOOM SAID, "I DISCOVERED THAT IT IS NOT ON OUR FORGIVENESS ANY MORE THAN ON OUR GOODNESS THAT THE WORLD'S HEALING HINGES, BUT ON HIS."

Jesus taught his disciples to pray, "Forgive us our debts, as we also have forgiven our debtors" (Matthew 6:12). Augustine labeled this request "the terrible petition" because if we pray this while withholding forgiveness from another, we ask God to not forgive us. Yet this prayer has a tremendous way of softening our hearts. As Corrie Ten Boom said, "I discovered that it is not on our forgiveness any more than on our goodness that the world's healing hinges, but on his. When he tells us to love our enemies, he gives, along with the command, the love itself."

One woman wrote to Dear Abby about the liberation of forgiveness. When she had just given birth to her fourth child (who became ill), her husband of ten years declared he didn't love her anymore and left. The woman couldn't eat or sleep, lost forty-seven pounds, became addicted to tranquilizers, and finally, had a nervous breakdown. Her husband returned only to put her in a mental hospital; then he had an affair with the woman's best friend.

After four months, her husband ended the affair. The other woman went back to her own husband and three children. And the letter writer decided to forgive her husband. She received counseling, went to church, and continued her Bible reading. She got off the pills and regained her family. She also forgave her friend, and they cried together and talked for six hours. In concluding her letter, she wrote:

> Forgiveness, when it is least deserved, has true healing power. In forgiving her, I released her of all her guilt and now God is able to work in my life. I feel a little insecure at times but I'm much better today than I was six months ago because a life filled with thoughts of revenge and bitterness is no life at all.

As difficult as forgiveness is, "a life filled with thoughts of revenge and bitterness is no life at all." This woman not only forgave, she took responsibility for her own destructive actions. Her husband took responsibility for walking out and having an affair. Eventually, this woman's friend also took responsibility. Her forgiveness did not mean she would not struggle to trust. It might take years to rebuild trust, yet she had discovered the power of forgiveness. If she experienced forgiveness after being wronged at this deep level, you too can discover the freedom of forgiveness in your relationship. So let God help you and "give a little bit." You'll never regret it.

What has your spouse done that you currently need to forgive?

PLAYLIST
No. **5**

MAKING LOVE LAST

Wink and a Smile

Marriage can be stressful because life is stressful—long commutes, piling bills, parenting issues, unreturned phone calls, strained family situations. Life is full of challenges, obstacles, and difficulties, often presenting themselves at the least expected times. The way we respond to and deal with challenges determines much about our own joy.

We've seen Solomon and the Shulammite go through a lot. As the Song continues they reflect on a maturing love and commitment. Time has not taken away their sense of adventure and celebration. She says, "Come, my lover, let us go to the countryside, let us spend the night in the villages. Let us go early to the vineyards to see if the vines have budded, if their blossoms have opened, and if the pomegranates are in bloom—there I will give you my love" (7:11, 12).

MY MOM ALWAYS SAID, "WHEN YOU ARE AT YOUR WIT'S END, YOU HAVE A CHOICE BETWEEN LAUGHING, CRYING, OR GOING NUTS; CHOOSE LAUGHTER."

They spontaneously went on a vacation to the countryside, choosing to keep their love alive and vibrant. We know they had their challenges, baggage, and pain, but they pushed through it all. To pull off love like that, they learned to laugh at the stupid things they did, at the odd things they said. Just think for a moment how weird it must be to live with you—and laugh. We all have our quirks. The grass isn't greener on the other side of the fence; it's just a different shade of yellow. And the "perfect couple" down the street face plenty of issues. Keep laughing, and keep pressing on. My mom always said, "When you are at your wit's end, you have a choice between laughing, crying, or going nuts; choose laughter."

"BE JOYFUL ALWAYS; PRAY CONTINUALLY; GIVE THANKS IN ALL CIRCUMSTANCES, FOR THIS IS GOD'S WILL FOR YOU IN CHRIST JESUS."

My friend Mark[34] and his spouse learned to laugh and enjoy themselves through hard times. I first met Mark in a marriage seminar and was immediately impressed by his attitude. Two years prior, Mark was in his thirties with a new baby when he came down with pneumonia. He endured a host of medical complications from the pneumonia. With the exception of his heart, every one of his organs took its turn at shutting down during that time period. Though doctors lost all hope, he amazingly pulled through. But his illness had taken its toll. Keeping him alive meant addressing circulatory problems and amputating his arms at the elbows and his legs above the knees. Mark left the hospital six months later, a multiple amputee with a young baby and a mountain of challenges.

Today Mark and his wife are still together and growing. They refuse to be victims and instead choose to enjoy life. He even skydives. In a marriage seminar, I overhead someone say to him, "You and your wife are such an inspiration to us. You have *real* problems, and you face them with courage." Mark was quick to correct him. "No," he said. "Your problems are just as real and challenging as ours. They are different, but still problems—we all have them. We all have to find ways to work through them and move forward."

What a view on life! God never hides the fact that life will have its problems, but throughout the Bible we are urged to choose joy and gladness. Paul says, "Be joyful always; pray continually; give thanks in all circumstances, for this is God's will for you in Christ Jesus" (1 Thessalonians 5:16-18). Happiness is a choice. It's an attitude within your grasp. You can discover God's desire for your relationship and experience his love and goodness in ways you never thought possible. Live with a "wink and a smile." Keep celebrating, laughing, and growing.

Plan something this week during which you can laugh together.

Return to Sender

One of Elvis's signature songs, "Return to Sender," tells the story of unreturned love. It describes love letters, romantic cards, poems, and (no doubt) apologies galore returned unopened to their sender. You can only understand the true heartache and pain of unreturned love if you've been the sender. God understands that feeling well. He continually sends love messages to his people that are sent back unopened. But if we want our relationships to go the distance, then we have to listen to those messages and put God first in our lives, including in our relationships.

Rob and Sue learned this lesson after much difficulty. When they first started dating, he would go to church with her, something he never did before they met. He was baptized, mainly to please her, and she thought this would make everything all right. Yet a month after the wedding, he quit going to church. For the next several years, things went downhill. He drank a lot, and he was a mean drunk. His favorite line became, "If you don't like it you can leave, because I'm not going to change." She continually prayed he would become a Christian, understanding it was the only hope for their marriage. Each Sunday for the next fifteen years she got their two children ready and took them to church. Sue said, "I was so hurt for so many years; then I didn't hurt anymore. I became numb inside. I built up this wall around my heart, so no matter what he did, it wouldn't hurt me."

One day Rob heard on the radio about a Christian men's retreat and to the complete shock of his wife, he went. He called her the first night of the retreat and said that though he couldn't explain it, he had changed inside; Jesus was in his heart. Sue simply said, "OK." She didn't believe him. She had heard so many empty words from him before— promises to change that were always broken.

But when Rob got home, the first thing he did was gather his family in one room. He apologized for the hurt he had caused and promised that with God's help he would change. It was a promise he kept.

Several years later Sue says, "Today, he remains one of the strongest and most faithful Christians I know. Our marriage isn't perfect, but we are working on it. He still has some bad habits, and I am trying to open my heart to him and forget the past. We are able to do this with God's help." God led them through a difficult time, just as he led Solomon and the Shulammite.

YOU CAN ONLY UNDERSTAND THE TRUE HEARTACHE AND PAIN OF UNRETURNED LOVE IF YOU'VE BEEN THE SENDER. GOD UNDERSTANDS THAT FEELING WELL.

In the Song of Solomon, one of the friends asks, "Who is this coming up from the desert leaning on her lover?" (8:5). Does that sound familiar? Remember in chapter 3, the Shulammite talks of her bridal procession and of seeing Solomon come out of the desert. In our discussion of that passage, we saw a connection to the story of the Israelites wandering in the desert, as found in the book of Exodus. God led this people with a pillar of cloud by day and a pillar of fire by night. This imagery, ingrained in Hebrew culture, being used here implies the presence of God once again. The Shulammite had described Solomon as coming up from the desert "like a column of smoke" (3:5). Now as they come together, side by side, she is "leaning on her lover," which shows an attitude of ease and trust. Solomon and the Shulammite have survived a time of difficulty, conflict, and pain in their relationship. The desert imagery reminds us that God has led them out of the wilderness just as he led the Israelites.

God is in the business of bringing people through wilderness experiences as they put their trust in him. One woman wrote me the following letter about letting God be the center of her marriage:

> When my husband and I first began attending church, our marriage was in poor shape. Sunday mornings were the only times we laughed for many months. God was not the major focus of our lives. Then my husband was in a bizarre accident and suffered a brain injury. Life changed in an instant, but God was there, working his miracles. The doctors didn't expect my husband to live, but he did. They didn't expect him to recover from the brain damage, but he has. My husband's recovery is not complete by any means, but his sense of humor surfaced early on. At that point I knew I could live with whatever lies ahead. Our marriage was once on the rocks. Through tragedy it has grown and strengthened in ways that continue to amaze me. My husband and I have since become members of God's family. I've discovered a wellspring of hope deep in my heart that gives me strength through endless dark nights, and the faith of knowing God is always with me. I am not alone in the journey. Faith now sustains me and brightens my darkest days.

GOD IS IN THE BUSINESS OF BRINGING PEOPLE THROUGH WILDERNESS EXPERIENCES AS THEY PUT THEIR TRUST IN HIM.

In God she found a "wellspring of hope." He can lead you through your own desert if you will depend on him. He loves you *more* than anyone else, and he loved you *before* anyone else. Return to the first sender of love; return to God.

> Talk with your spouse about where God is in your marriage. What are some practical steps you can take to get your focus on God right?

Livin' on a Prayer

Bon Jovi's "Livin' on a Prayer" became a huge smash and was performed before a televised audience of over sixty million as part of the "Tribute to My Heroes" telethon for the victims of 9/11. But it almost didn't make the album *Slippery When Wet*. It wasn't until Jon Bon Jovi played it for some teenagers and heard their comments that he changed his mind about including it on the record. The song chronicles the journey of Tommy and Gina, two young kids trying to make their way against all sorts of challenges.[35]

Irrespective of how things are going, we should all be livin' on a prayer. One couple who did just that sent me a letter, which I found inspiring. She wrote of the hard times they had experienced in their marriage. Things came to a head, and she and her husband separated. Afterward they both separately began attending church. Eventually they chose to meet in a neutral spot, a park near their home. She writes, "There we sat apart from one another at a picnic table, tears flooding both our eyes. You could see that both of us were wondering what the other was thinking, and the big question remained: where do we go from here? We talked about everything, from every emotion we had been feeling to how hurt we were from what had happened."

As they said good-bye, they faced an awkward moment. "It felt like we were in high school together," she writes. "Do we shake hands? Do we hug? Do we kiss? We don't know where the relationship is."

In that moment her husband did something that she didn't expect. He held his hand out and said, "Let's pray." For the first time in their relationship, her husband prayed for their marriage. She writes, "This is a date that I will never forget." It was a powerful moment in their lives and in their relationship. Prayer can help us discover God in the wilderness times.

TOO OFTEN PRAYER IS OUR LAST RESORT.

We've seen Solomon and the Shulammite come through tough times. We've seen conflict erupt and real injury happen, but we've also seen God leading them through the wilderness. "Who is this coming up from the desert leaning on her lover?" (8:5). As we lean on each other and on God, we come through the difficult times. We are renewed, like the Shulammite, in the realization that we belong to each other: "I belong to my lover, and his desire is for me" (7:10).

Prayer is an essential part of experiencing God, following his leading in our lives and in our marriages. Too often prayer is our last resort. We wait for a crisis and then cry out to God in anguish, wondering where he is in all of it. Maybe he's wondering why it took so long to get our attention. God longs for us to come to him in prayer. One of the reasons I think we don't pray more often is that we've become addicted to the concept of IG—Instant Gratification. We live in a world where we can get what we want when we want it, without waiting. Microwaves, credit cards, liposuction, McDonald's . . . All these things reflect our impatience. Any company that can reduce the amount of time between our wanting a thing and having the thing tends to be successful. IG isn't bad, it's just that not every experience in life is instantly gratifying. Prayer is in the realm of IGT—In God's Time. God always hears the instant we pray, but sometimes the answer or the response occurs over time. This is God's mercy.

Ever prayed for something to happen that didn't come about? Particularly in a marriage, prayer doesn't always lead to an immediate fix. It is easy to take a fatalistic view and assume prayer changes nothing, but Jesus never referred to an unanswered prayer in his teaching. He answers prayer, but he answers according to his character and timetable, not ours. God loves to answer prayer for our benefit.

Jesus teaches this when he asks, "Which of you, if his son asks for bread, will give him a stone? Or if he asks for a fish, will give him a snake? If you, then, though you are evil, know how to give good gifts to your children, how much more will your Father in heaven give good gifts to those who ask him!" (Matthew 7:9-11).

"IF YOU, THEN, THOUGH YOU ARE EVIL, KNOW HOW TO GIVE GOOD GIFTS TO YOUR CHILDREN, HOW MUCH MORE WILL YOUR FATHER IN HEAVEN GIVE GOOD GIFTS TO THOSE WHO ASK HIM!"

God is a loving Father who gives good gifts. He answers prayer with your best interest in mind, which is why he sometimes says no. If a child asks for bread, that is one thing; if he asks to put his hand in the fire, that is another. The child doesn't realize what will happen, but the father has to say no. That is how God is with us. Pastor and author Bill Hybels shares this formula: "If the request is wrong, God says, 'No.' If the timing is wrong, God says, 'Slow.' If you are wrong, God says, 'Grow.' And if the request is right, the timing is right, and you are right, God says, 'Go.'"[36] God answers prayer, but he does so in his own mysterious way.

God knows what is best for you and for your marriage. So think about what your marriage needs right now. Then lay your needs before him. He wants nothing more than for you to come boldly before him, "livin' on a prayer."

Take some time and pray together about the needs in your lives and in your relationship.

A Man and a Woman

U2's "A Man and a Woman" is a powerful testimony to mature love. In the song, Bono contrasts committed love with fleeting romance and comments that he will not throw love away for a quick fling. After more than two decades of marriage to the same woman, Bono knows the benefits of a long-term relationship.

It's common today for couples to make a visit to an attorney's office before walking down the aisle. Men and women with established careers and acquired wealth and assets seek financial protection through prenuptial agreements and marriage contracts. But contracts and agreements are broken every day.

Actor Mel Gibson tells a story about talking with an older man about marriage. "We were having a real heart-to-heart," recalls Gibson, "then his wife appeared. She was a beautiful girl about nineteen or twenty. And I said, 'Oh, you are a lucky man.' The man shook his head and answered, 'I should have stayed with my first wife. Things haven't changed—she just looks different.'" Gibson concludes, "You see, people are chasing things they can't get. They're just illusions. You've got to make a commitment in marriage—just say, 'This is it.' I think too many people go into marriage too lightly. You've got to take it seriously—go in there to make it last."[37]

God designed marriage as a lasting covenant. In ancient times, a covenant was much more than a legal agreement. It was made before

God, with a penalty of death for breaking it. In his book *The Marriage Masterpiece*, author Al Janssen draws four parallels between a covenant ceremony in the Bible and a marriage ceremony: 1) Both are conducted with God as witness; 2) In each case human witnesses must be present for a valid ceremony; 3) At both ceremonies, the presiding officiator reads a statement declaring the seriousness of the commitment; and finally, 4) The parties involved always exchange something of value. Janssen writes,

> It particularly struck me when I read the words uttered by the husband when he places the wedding ring on his wife's finger, "With this ring I thee wed, with my body I thee worship, and with all my worldly goods I thee endow." In other words, the husband gave everything he had to his wife, including his body and his earthly possessions. No longer were there his or her possessions. Everything was theirs. Why is this important? Because in giving our all, we actually gain what we want.[38]

Solomon and his bride understood the concept of giving their all. As we read through the Song of Solomon, there are continual reminders of how passionately they loved each other, invested in each other, and kept the romance burning. The Shulammite says, "Under the apple tree I roused you; there your mother conceived you, there she who was in labor gave you birth" (8:5). She is not literally saying she roused him at the apple tree that he was conceived under. The term "apple tree" is used earlier as a reference to Solomon; here it refers to his father. Solomon's father and mother were physically intimate, and Solomon was conceived. Now she and Solomon engage in the same intimacy. Though time has passed, it has not diminished their passion.

It's like the elderly couple lying in bed one night. She rolled over and said, "When we were younger, you used to hold my hand at night." There was a long pause. Then he reached over and took her hand.

She said, "When we were younger, we used to cuddle together at night." Another pause. He slid over next to her and cuddled up.

She said, "When we were younger, you nibbled on my ear at night." Suddenly he threw the covers off, got out of bed, and began to leave the room. She was stung by his action. "Where are you going?" she asked.

"I'm going to get my teeth!" he replied.

BECAUSE IN GIVING OUR ALL, WE ACTUALLY GAIN WHAT WE WANT.

The Song of Solomon challenges us to keep the fires burning in our marriage, even if it means getting out of bed to get your teeth. The passion of Solomon and his bride is evident on every page, but their commitment goes far beyond passion. She says, "Place me like a seal over your heart, like a seal on your arm; for love is as strong as death, its jealousy unyielding as the grave. It burns like blazing fire, like a mighty flame" (8:6). A seal in this culture marked something as being possessed by another, denoting ownership and security. In saying "place me like a seal over your heart," she completely gives herself to him. One version of this verse reads, "Wear me as a signet ring on your heart; as a ring on your hand" (8:6, *GW*). The signet ring functioned as a signature and was worn on one's finger. It represented a pledge or guarantee of full payment. When Solomon and his wife gave themselves to each other in this way, each had free possession of the other's life. They belonged to one another.

That commitment is anchored in the power of God. The Song says love "burns like blazing fire, like a mighty flame." Some translations include the phrase "mighty flame of the Lord," because in the original language the last syllable of the word *flame* used here could refer to God's name.

God's idea of commitment and covenant includes each party making a permanent vow. Today's culture places high value on personal happiness, freedom, and independence. You may bristle at the thought of giving yourself fully and completely to your spouse. The permanence of covenant may leave you feeling boxed in. But let's broaden that perspective from our own frame of reference to God's overall view.

"PLACE ME LIKE A SEAL OVER YOUR HEART, LIKE A SEAL ON YOUR ARM; FOR LOVE IS AS STRONG AS DEATH."

God offers greater security and freedom to grow through our dependence on each other. Marriage offers a safe haven in which to boldly plan and pursue goals and a future together. Joy comes when you support each other along the way, share burdens, and celebrate each other's victories. Problems will come and go. You will face trials, have disagreements, and differ in opinions, but you will always know you have each other, without a doubt. That's the kind of commitment we enter into when we exchange rings and vows. God's concept of covenant between a man and a woman is a commitment of everlasting love, a marriage relationship that goes the distance. Give yourselves completely to one another and see how far God will take you.

Is there an area you are holding back from your spouse? If so, how can you share that?

Everything I Do

New Year's Eve, 1984. A grocery store. 11:00 PM.

Enter stage left: Julie. Staggering half drunk down the aisle, she pushes a cart full of party snacks, cigarettes, and alcohol. She is in a hurry to get back to her friends, down a few more drinks, and ring in the New Year in the usual fashion—plastered.

Enter stage right: Steve. Alone on New Year's Eve for the first time in years, he finds himself wandering the aisles of the grocery store. He is lost in his thoughts and is feeling he has little reason to celebrate.

Each looks up and sees the other, a distant but familiar face. A conversation ensues.

In the decade since Julie last saw Steve Sanders, she had endured three failed marriages, financial instability, and the responsibilities of being a single parent. Her drinking helped ease the pressures, but failed to dull the agony of her past. It was destroying every aspect of her life. Hopelessness and sorrow were overtaking any love remaining in her heart.

"THE LESS IMPORTANT YOU MAKE YOURSELF, THE HAPPIER YOU ARE."

Steve, too, was a man in pain. He was in the midst of divorce after suffering years of verbal abuse in his marriage. But Steve was also a dedicated Christian man. He sensed Julie's condition and the direction her life had taken. So right there and then, with genuine concern, Steve asked Julie about her drinking. She left the grocery store upset and in denial about her problem.

As unlikely as it was, that night marked the beginning of an awesome relationship. Julie and her children began attending the church where Steve led the choir, and eventually each accepted Christ as forgiver and leader. The family transformed as Christ became the center of their hearts. And a couple years later, Steve and Julie celebrated New Year's Eve in that same grocery store as husband and wife.

The story of Steve and Julie Sanders is a great story of redemption, forgiveness, and the amazing way God mends broken lives and hearts. But that's not why I'm telling it. Because what happens next is even better. Steve and Julie have developed one of the greatest marriages of any couple I have ever known, and people are drawn to them like magnets. God uses them powerfully as a refuge for hurting couples.

I sat down with Steve and Julie to ask them how they achieved such a great marriage. Steve said, "We treat each other as being more important than ourselves. When you give up your own personal rights willingly, and both of you are doing it, it really works great." They strive to keep Christ as the center of their focus, conversation, and thoughts.

Steve and Julie attribute their wonderful marriage to God and an attitude of service. Their marriage foundation rests on Philippians 2:2, 3: "Make my joy complete by being like-minded, having the same love, being one in spirit and purpose. Do nothing out of selfish ambition or vain conceit, but in humility consider others better than yourselves." This is the theme of their lives.

Their advice to married couples is anchored in Jesus' idea, "If you lose your life, you'll find it." Steve says, "That works in marriage as it does in every other aspect of your life. The less important you make yourself, the happier you are."

Solomon and the Shulammite also represent a serving attitude. She reflects back on how they met and on the priority they've given to each other. She says: "I have become in his eyes like one bringing contentment. Solomon had a vineyard in Baal Hamon; he let out his vineyard to tenants. Each was to bring for its fruit a thousand shekels of silver. But my own vineyard is mine to give; the thousand shekels are for you, O Solomon . . ." (8:10-12). Reflecting on that day they first met, she acknowledges that her vineyard, her own self, is hers to give, and she gives it to Solomon completely. Everything, including her income (a thousand shekels), she gives to him. She is the one who brings him contentment. She serves him completely.

If you want amazing transformation in your relationship, start by trying to outserve your spouse. Pastor and speaker Wellington Boone tells of a period of time when he noticed his wife doing all kinds of nice things for him. She was tireless in her service to him. One day he realized she was serving God by serving him. So he then began throwing himself into serving her, declaring, "You will not outserve me!" Talk about a little friendly competition! Boone says, "Our marriage works because we're not trying to make each other happy; we're trying to make God happy. And we make him happy by treating each other like he treats us."

IF YOU WANT AMAZING TRANSFORMATION IN YOUR RELATIONSHIP, START BY TRYING TO OUTSERVE YOUR SPOUSE.

Great marriage relationships don't just happen. They require attention, work, and play. So build on the foundation of God's Word and grow in your relationship with him. Let everything you do be for God, and thus, for your spouse as well. Compete to outserve your spouse, and build a marriage that lasts.

What's one practical thing you can do today to serve your spouse?

Grow Old with Me

One family decided to honor their parents' long and devoted commitment to marriage by throwing them a 50th wedding anniversary party. In the course of events, the husband stood to make a toast to his wife. Lifting his glass he said, "My dear wife, after fifty years I've found you tried and true." Everyone smiled with approval except his wife who had trouble hearing. She cupped a hand behind her ear and said, "Eh?" Her husband repeated himself loudly, "AFTER FIFTY YEARS I'VE FOUND YOU TRIED AND TRUE!" Without missing a beat, his wife shot back, "Well, let me tell YOU something—after fifty years I'm tired of you too!"

In your mind's eye, can you picture those two a half century ago as a young couple just crazy in love? We start out in marriage as two distinct individuals with a fever-like passion for each other. Along with the passion of intimacy, early marriages have passionate disagreements. Young couples may slam doors, hang up on each other, run home and tattle to their parents, and do all kinds of crazy things during a fiery dispute. The good news for newlyweds is that they can settle into marriage, learn to compromise, and get comfortable with each other's differences. The bad news is that arguing is not the only place where passions may dwindle over time. It takes effort to keep stoking the flames of romance as the years tick by, children enter the picture, and responsibilities increase.

Have you ever noticed how longtime couples take on the language, attributes, and personality traits of each other? They even begin to look like each other over time. Steve Lawrence and Eydie Gorme are a singing duo, married for many, many years. They were friends with Frank Sinatra, Tony Bennett, and all the old great crooners. So they'll often be interviewed together to share stories or memories of the old days. I'm not sure if either one of them is capable of telling a story without the other. It's hilarious to watch them. One starts a sentence and the other finishes. They go back and forth as if they are one person relating the tale. Have you ever been around a couple like that?

"MANY WATERS CANNOT QUENCH LOVE; RIVERS CANNOT WASH IT AWAY."

In the Song of Solomon, we've looked at snapshots and vignettes of the life and relationship of such a couple, Solomon and his wife, the Shulammite. Picture them now, sitting side by side with their box of memories. They've thickened at the waist a bit and have a few laugh lines, and they both have a spray of silver at the temples. Through this collection of love poems, they've generously opened the book on their relationship, sharing the most crucial elements with us.

First came their dialogue about the nature of love in chapters 1 and 2. Next, chapter 3 described their wedding night. Then we learned about sexuality and intimacy in chapter 4. Chapters 5 and 6 portrayed relational conflict and the necessity of working through life's inevitable trials. Now we see the value of lifetime commitment and God's design for marriage.

Lifetime commitment means remaining faithful in tough times. The Song of Solomon says, "Many waters cannot quench love; rivers cannot wash it away" (8:7). Every marriage faces rough waters, but love will not wash away. My dad is a WWII vet, and I'm the youngest of four children. My dad never finished high school because he went right into the war. After the war he fell in love with my mom, and they scraped by with very little money. At their one-year anniversary, my dad had only one dime to his name, but he wanted to do something to celebrate. So he went to the store and bought all he could afford, a Hershey bar for my mom. He took it to her and said, "Honey, it's not much, but I'll add one Hershey bar for every year we are together. I'll serve you and love you for the rest of my life." Last year, my dad bought fifty-nine Hershey bars for my mom. There was never a shortage of chocolate in our household. It was a constant reminder that money can buy a lot, but love is priceless. As the Shulammite says, "If one were to give all the wealth of his house for love, it would be utterly scorned" (8:7).

It's the little things that make love last, the small daily commitments and minor inconveniences cheerfully endured. These are the bricks that build a strong marriage through the years. Paul Brand, a missionary doctor who worked for many years among leprosy victims in India, said, "As I enter my sixth decade of marriage I can say without a flicker of hesitation that the basic human virtue of faithfulness to one partner is the most joyful way of life. . . . I have always trusted my wife completely, and she me. We have each been able to channel love and commitment and intimacy to one person—a lifelong investment that is now, in old age, paying rich dividends."[39]

IT'S THE LITTLE THINGS THAT MAKE LOVE LAST, THE SMALL DAILY COMMITMENTS AND MINOR INCONVENIENCES CHEERFULLY ENDURED.

As the music fades on this soundtrack of marriage, sex, and faith, I pray you'll continue incorporating these principles into your life.

When you shelve this book, don't shelve your relationship. Remember the crazy feeling of love you felt when you courted? Guys, the way you won her is the way you will keep her. Continue to pursue her and serve her. And ladies, keep pouring into him. Meet his needs and invest in your relationship so it becomes all that God desires it to be. Start with small steps and know that God will do great things in your marriage. Through love and commitment to your spouse, one day you will be able to reflect on your lifelong investment in each other and enjoy the rich dividends. It's a crazy, wonderful thought, isn't it?

Commit to invest in your marriage on a regular basis by reading, talking, dating, and meeting each other's needs.

About the Author

Jud Wilhite is senior pastor of Central Christian Church, a pioneering and creative community of faith in the Las Vegas area. Over 10,000 attend Central's campuses each weekend. Jud is the author of several books including *Faith That Goes the Distance*. A creative partner with Pursuit.org, he lives in the Las Vegas area with his wife, Lori, and their two children.

A portion of the proceeds from *That Crazy Little Thing Called Love* will go to Corps of Compassion to help feed hungry and homeless children in the Las Vegas Valley (www.jointhecorps.org).

Notes

[1] Adapted from Chuck Missler, *The Book of Song of Songs: A Commentary*, an audiotape of a message presented for Koinonia House (Koinonia House, 2001).

[2] *The New Bible Commentary, The Scholars Library* (Bellingham, WA: Logos Bible Software, 2004).

[3] Henry Morris, *The Remarkable Wisdom of Solomon: Ancient Insights from the Song of Solomon, Proverbs, and Ecclesiastes* (Green Forest, AR: Masterbooks, 2001), 27–32, 35–36.

[4] John Gottman and Nan Silver, *The Seven Principles of Making Marriage Work* (New York: Three Rivers, 1999), 64.

[5] Emerson Eggerichs, *Love and Respect: The Love She Most Desires, the Respect He Desperately Needs* (Brentwood, TN: Integrity, 1994), 47.

[6] Ibid., 49.

[7] Ibid., 189.

[8] "Have I Told You Lately That I Love You?" *Songfacts,* http://www.songfacts.com/detail.php?id=1308.

[9] Gary Chapman, *The Five Love Languages: How to Express Heartfelt Commitment to Your Mate* (Chicago: Northfield Publishing, 1995).

[10] John Gottman with Nan Silver, *Why Marriages Succeed or Fail . . . And How You Can Make Yours Last* (New York: Simon and Schuster, 1994), 57.

[11] Marcus Buckingham, *The One Thing You Need to Know ... About Great Managing, Great Leading and Sustained Individual Success* (New York: Free Press, 2005), 22.

[12] "Seven Ages of a Married Cold," *Saturday Evening Post,* as quoted in Skip Heitzig, *Relationships: Connecting the Knots in the Threads of Life* (Albuquerque, NM: Connection Communications, 1998), 85–86.

[13] E. V. Hill, as quoted in Eggerichs, *Love and Respect*, 211.

[14] "'Stand By Your Man' Tops Song List," *CBS News,* 5 June 2003, www.cbsnews.com/stories/2003/06/05/entertainment/main557119.shtml.

[15] "National Health and Social Life Survey," *The Journal of the American Medical Association*, 1999.

[16] Rabbi Nachmanides, as quoted in Ruth Westheimer and Jonathon Mark, "The Jewish View of Sex," *Generation J*, 18 April 2005, http://jewish.com/modules.php?name=News.

[17] Shaunti Feldhahn, *For Women Only: What You Need to Know About the Inner Lives of Men* (Sisters, OR: Multnomah, 2004), 98.

[18] Ibid., 163.

[19] See Ed and Lisa Young, *4Keeps: Keeping Creativity in Your Marriage* (Keller, TX: On Purpose Media, 2000), 84.

[20] As quoted in Lorraine Ali and Lisa Miller, "The New Infidelity," *Newsweek,* 12 July 2004, http://msnbc.msn.com/id/5550736/site/newsweek.

[21] Dawn Lipthrott, "60 Starter Ideas to Have an Affair with Your Spouse/Partner," *The Relationship Learning Center*, www.relationshipjourney.com/affair.html.

[22] See Ed and Lisa Young, *4Keeps,* 77–78. I

adapted Willard Harley's illustration.

23 Jill Eggleton Brett, "Not Tonight, Dear . . ." *Today's Christian Woman* 24, no. 2 (March/April 2002): 68, quoted in Feldhahn, *For Women Only,* 105–106.

24 *See* Gary Thomas, *Sacred Marriage* (Grand Rapids: Zondervan, 2000), 80.

25 Jimmy Evans, *Marriage on the Rock: God's Design for Your Dream Marriage* (Amarillo, TX: Majestic Media, 1994), 257.

26 John Gottman as quoted in Malcolm Gladwell, *Blink: The Power of Thinking Without Thinking* (New York: Little Brown and Company, 2005), 32–33.

27 Eddie Schwartz, "Hit Me With Your Best Shot," *Songfacts,* http://www.songfacts.com/detail.php?id=1403.

28 Gottman, *The Seven Principles,* 130.

29 Dan Wile, as quoted in Gottman, *The Seven Principles,* 131–132.

30 Gottman, *The Seven Principles,* 27.

31 Neil Jacobson, as quoted in Gottman, *The Seven Principles,* 10.

32 Tommy Nelson, *The Book of Romance: What Solomon Says About Love, Sex and Romance* (Nashville: Thomas Nelson, 1999), 125–126.

33 Roger Hodgson, "Interpretation of Lyrics for 'Give a Little Bit,'" *Kid's Help Out Online,* http://www.kidshelpout.org/learn/lyric.html.

34 All names and some details in this story and others in the book have been changed to protect the identities of those involved.

35 From "Livin' on a Prayer," *Songfacts,* http://www.songfacts.com/detail.php?id=1148.

36 Bill Hybels, *Too Busy Not To Pray* (Downers Grove, IL: InterVarsity Press, 1988), 74.

37 Mel Gibson, as quoted in Phil Callaway, *Making Life Rich Without Any Money* (Eugene, OR: Harvest House, 1998), www.family.org/married/comm/a0020156.cfm.

38 Al Janssen, *The Marriage Masterpiece* (Wheaton, IL: Tyndale House, 2001), www.family.org/married/comm/a0017718.cfm.

39 Paul Brand, as quoted in Callaway, *Making Life Rich,* www.family.org/married/comm/a0020156.cfm.

Crazy Little Song List

INTRO: **Crazy Little Thing Called Love**
Words and music by Freddie Mercury. Performed by Freddie Mercury and Queen.

1. **Beautiful**
Words, music, and performance by Billy Corgan.

2. **R-E-S-P-E-C-T**
Words and music by Otis Redding. Performed by Aretha Franklin.

3. **Have I Told You Lately?**
Words and music by Van Morrison. Performed by Rod Stewart.

4. **Girls Just Want to Have Fun**
Words and music by Robert Hazard. Performed by Cyndi Lauper.

5. **Tell Her About It**
Words, music, and performance by Billy Joel.

6. **Chapel of Love**
Words and music by Jeff Barry, Ellie Greenwich, and Phil Spector. Performed by the Dixie Cups.

7. **I Only Have Eyes for You**
Words and music by Al Dubin and Harry Warren. Performed by the Flamingos.

8. **Where Is the Love?**
Performed by the Black Eyed Peas.

9. **Dedicated to the One I Love**
Words and music by Ralph Bass and Lowman Pauling. Performed by the Mamas and the Papas.

10. She Believes in Me

Words and music by Stephen M. Gibb. Performed by Kenny Rogers.

11. Stand by Your Man

Words and music by Tammy Wynette and Billy Sherrill. Performed by Tammy Wynette.

12. Love Me Tender

Words and music by Elvis Presley, Vera Matson, and Ken Darby. Performed by Elvis Presley.

13. I'm Too Sexy

Words, music, and performance by Right Said Fred.

14. In Your Eyes

Words, music, and performance by Peter Gabriel.

15. Behind Closed Doors

Words and music by Charlie Rich and Billy Sherrill. Performed by Charlie Rich.

16. Wonderful Tonight

Words, music, and performance by Eric Clapton.

17. Celebration

Words, music, and performance by Kool & the Gang.

18. Emotional Rollercoaster

Words, music, and performance by Vivian Green.

19. Hit Me with Your Best Shot

Words and music by Eddie Schwartz. Performed by Pat Benatar.

20. Love Is a Battlefield

Words, music, and performance by Pat Benatar.

21. You Wreck Me
Words and music by Tom Petty. Performed by Tom Petty and the Heartbreakers.

22. Cuts Like a Knife
Words, music, and performance by Bryan Adams and Jim Vallance.

23. You've Got a Friend in Me
Words and music by Randy Newman. Performed by Randy Newman and Lyle Lovett.

24. Give a Little Bit
Words and music by Roger Hodgson. Performed by Roger Hodgson and Supertramp.

25. Wink and a Smile
Words and music by Marc Shaiman and Ramsey McLean. Performed by Harry Connick, Jr.

26. Return to Sender
Words and music by Otis Blackwell and Winfield Scott. Performed by Elvis Presley.

27. Livin' on a Prayer
Words and music by Jon Bon Jovi, Richie Sambora, and Desmond Child. Performed by Bon Jovi.

28. A Man and a Woman
Words, music, and performance by Bono and U2.

29. Everything I Do
Words and music by Bryan Adams, Mutt Lange, and Michael Kamen. Performed by Bryan Adams.

30. Grow Old with Me
Words, music, and performance by John Lennon.